Essay *on the* Nature *of* TRADE in General

Essay *on* *the* Nature *of* TRADE in General

RICHARD CANTILLON

Translated, Edited, and with an Introduction by

ANTOIN E. MURPHY

LIBERTY FUND *Indianapolis*

This book is published by Liberty Fund, Inc.,
a foundation established to encourage study of the
ideal of a society of free and responsible individuals.

⬚⬚ ⬚⬚

The cuneiform inscription that serves as our logo and as the design motif
for our endpapers is the earliest-known written appearance of the word
"freedom" (*amagi*), or "liberty." It is taken from a clay document written
about 2300 B.C. in the Sumerian city-state of Lagash.

19 18 17 16 15 C 5 4 3 2 1
19 18 17 16 15 P 5 4 3 2 1

Library of Congress Cataloging-in-Publication Data
Cantillon, Richard, –1734.
   [Éssai sur la nature du commerce en général. English]
   Essay on the nature of trade in general / Richard Cantillon; translated,
edited, and with an introduction by Antoin E. Murphy.
     pages   cm
   Translation of the author's Éssai sur la nature du commerce en général.
   Includes bibliographical references and index.
   ISBN 978-0-86597-874-4 (hardcover: alk. paper)—
   ISBN 978-0-86597-875-1 (pbk.: alk. paper)
   1. Economics. 2. Commerce. I. Title.
   HB153 .C313 2015b
   330—dc23   2015008456

LIBERTY FUND, INC.
8335 Allison Pointe Trail, Suite 300
Indianapolis, Indiana 46250-1684

CONTENTS

INTRODUCTION

Richard Cantillon's Background

In 1721, when the French authorities decided to introduce the Visa, a retrospective tax on those who had enriched themselves through John Law's Mississippi System, the world's first financial bubble, Richard Cantillon featured as one of the prominent millionaires. In the Visa's tax document he was classified in the first list of rich Mississippians for having allegedly made 20 million livres from his transactions in Mississippi paper. The tax imposed on him was 2.4 million livres. A further column in the tax document described the rich Mississippians. Here, intriguingly, the only comment that could be made about Richard Cantillon was that he was an unknown (*un inconnu*).[1] This comment was surprising because the so-called unknown Cantillon had been running a bank in Paris for at least six years and had been involved in some major financial transactions there. It may be conjectured that Cantillon, wishing to hide under the cover of anonymity, encouraged a Visa official to conceal details of his identity. Richard Cantillon was very much a man of mystery. He liked to cover his tracks, using at times the names of his cousin, the Chevalier Richard Cantillon, and his nephew, also called Richard Cantillon, as fronts for his banking operations. His date of birth is still not known, and he died under such mysterious circumstances, in London in 1734, that there is doubt as to whether it was his body that was burnt to ashes in the fire that engulfed his house. Thus Cantillon was very much an eighteenth-century enigma, a man capable of writing one of the greatest books on economics of that century, while at the same time gliding through the commercial, financial, political, and intellectual circles of Paris, London, and Amsterdam without attracting excessive attention.

Notwithstanding his desire for anonymity, he had mixed with some

---

1. See Du Hautchamp 1743, vol. 2, 170.

of the great figures of the period. He had been the key banker in dis-
counting a substantial bill of exchange amounting to £20,000 for Lord
Bolingbroke when he fled to Paris in 1715. Cantillon was sufficiently
confident to challenge Sir Isaac Newton about his report on the coinage when they met, probably in 1717, in Exchange Alley, London.[2] His
relationship with John Law, the creator of the Mississippi System, had
blown hot and cold. Initially they had been partners in a company to
colonize an area of French Louisiana; then Cantillon had been evicted
from France for speculating against the French currency and the shares
of the Mississippi System; and finally Law had invited him back to
France in the summer of 1720 to act as his assistant in restructuring the
Mississippi System, an invitation that Cantillon turned down. Along
with his wife, he was a friend of Montesquieu, although it is difficult
to know when they first met. He had the great French portraitist Ni-
colas Largillière paint his wife, while he himself sat on two occasions
for portraits by the Italian painter Rosalba Carrera.

Tracing Cantillon's lineage has been a difficult task. It has not been
possible to find a date of birth for Cantillon, though it is known that
he was born in Ballyronan, part of the parish of Ballyheigue, in the
northwestern part of County Kerry, Ireland. Cantillon's brother,
Thomas, is buried in the Ballyheigue churchyard. It may be surmised
that he was born between 1680 and 1690. He became a naturalized
Frenchman in 1708, which suggests that he may have done so on at-
taining the age of twenty-one. If this is the case, then Cantillon would
have been born in 1687.

His family originated in Normandy. It is believed that the name was
originally Chant-de-loup, "the cry of the wolf," which gradually became corrupted to Cantillon and Condon in Ireland. They appear to
have followed William the Conqueror to England and then later came
to Ireland under Henry II. Locating in County Kerry, they became
Hiberno/Norman lords of the manor until they were dispossessed of
their lands in the seventeenth century by the Cromwellian plantations
and the Williamite confiscations. Sometime after the Treaty of Limer-
ick in 1691, which ended hostilities in Ireland between the Williamites

2. See Cantillon 1931, ch. 4, book 3.

and Jacobites, Cantillon emigrated to France. His application for French naturalization, mentioned above, shows that he was in France by 1708.

Cantillon's uncle, Sir Daniel Arthur, was the Jacobites' banker. He had been instrumental in transferring the financial capital of the Irish Jacobites out of Ireland. This connection probably provided Cantillon with an introduction into the world of banking. He appears to have started this career by providing financial assistance for British prisoners of war during the War of the Spanish Succession. From France he traveled to Spain. The first known sighting of Cantillon in Spain was in 1712. Surprisingly for an Irish Catholic, forced from his ancestral lands by the Williamites, he was working on the British side during the final stages of the War of the Spanish Succession in the Iberian Peninsula.

Cantillon worked as a deputy to Anthony Hammond, the representative in Spain of the British Paymaster General to the Forces Abroad, James Brydges.[3] Brydges, who later became Lord Carnarvon and still later the Duke of Chandos, was the biggest war profiteer of the age.

Working for Chandos, Cantillon became adept at the art of double-double-entry bookkeeping, maintaining an official set of books for parliament and a private set for Chandos, revealing the full extent of his profit-making activities. Cantillon's financial efficiency impressed Chandos to such an extent that he offered Cantillon employment in London and also gave him a loan of £2,000. Cantillon rejected the employment offer, preferring to travel to Paris to take over the banking practice of his cousin the Chevalier Richard Cantillon. He also quickly paid off Chandos's loan, suggesting that he was able to turn the chevalier's virtually bankrupt banking operation into a profitable one relatively quickly.

By 1717 Cantillon had encountered a man who was to have a profound effect on the rest of his career. This was the Scotsman John Law (1671–1729), who had started to implement his grand design aimed at transforming the French monetary and financial systems.[4] Law believed that France faced dual crises. The first was a monetary crisis exemplified by the shortage of money in France. The second was a

3. See Baker and Baker 1949.
4. See Murphy 1997.

financial crisis in the form of massive government indebtedness brought on by the excessive expenditures of the late king Louis XIV to finance the wars that he had waged. Law believed that he could solve the monetary crisis by establishing a note-issuing bank, while he aimed to resolve the financial crisis by converting the public debt into equity of a trading company, which would later become known as the Mississippi Company. These policies of monetary expansion and debt restructuring were the two main pillars of John Law's Mississippi System. Law developed his system progressively by establishing in 1716 the General Bank, later to become the Royal Bank, to issue banknotes. Following this he revamped the Company of the West (Compagnie d'Occident) to become the base for the creation of a vast financial conglomerate that controlled all the French trading companies, the mint, the tobacco farms, and the tax farms. The Company of the West controlled the trading rights to French Louisiana, a vast expanse of territory in North America constituting half of the land mass of the present United States, if Alaska is excluded. The shares issued by this company rose from a price of around 170 livres on issue in 1717 to a high of over 10,000 livres at the end of 1719 and the start of 1720. Law's alchemist qualities in transforming paper money and shares into apparent wealth led to his appointment as Controller General of Finances in France, a role equivalent to that of prime minister, in January 1720 at the height of the Mississippi Bubble, which was generated by the Mississippi System.

Cantillon's relationship with Law varied from friendship to enmity during the Mississippi System episode. Initially they were on sufficiently good terms to establish, along with Joseph Gage, one of the biggest Mississippian speculators, a colonizing group to develop a settlement in Louisiana. Cantillon's brother Bernard led this group from La Rochelle to New Orleans in 1719.

When the shares in the Mississippi Company rose from 170 to over 2,000 livres in the early summer of 1719, Cantillon became convinced that a definite asset market bubble had emerged. He sold his shares and retired to Italy in August 1719. Cantillon's timing was wrong, as the Mississippi Company moved from strength to strength. By January 1720, the shares had moved to over 10,000 livres.

Cantillon returned to France in the spring of 1720. Then, convinced more than ever that the Mississippi System would explode, he shorted the shares of the company and the French currency. Law became aware of Cantillon's bearish activities and threatened him with the Bastille if he did not leave France within forty-eight hours. Cantillon did so but continued to speculate against the company and the French currency from his bases in London and Amsterdam.

Believing that a similar bubble emanating from speculation in South Sea Company shares had emerged in Britain, Cantillon took out sizable put option contracts with Dutch bankers on the British shares. Meanwhile, in France, when the Mississippi Company faced increasing difficulties in the early summer of 1720, John Law invited Cantillon to return to France to assist him in restructuring the system. Cantillon turned down the offer, fearing that his profits, made through shorting the company's shares and the French currency, would be confiscated when the system eventually collapsed. By the end of 1720 Law was forced to flee from France as his system collapsed. Cantillon, on the other hand, had made a considerable fortune, but he was to find that there were costs associated with making his fortune. Some of his clients, led by Lady Mary Herbert and Joseph Gage, were responsible for criminal and civil suits against him alleging that he shorted the Mississippi System with shares that they had given him as collateral for loans. These charges were never proven, but they did mean that Cantillon faced continuous litigation in both Britain and France for the rest of his life.

Richard Cantillon married Mary Anne O'Mahony (1701–51) in February 1722. She was also of Kerry stock, being the daughter of Count Daniel O'Mahony, who had been born in Killarney, County Kerry. Mary Anne was regarded by her contemporaries, such as Lady Mary Wortley Montagu, as one of the beauties of her age.

Cantillon was apparently murdered in his bed in Albemarle Street, London, on May 14, 1734, by his disgruntled French cook, who then set fire to the house. The corpse was burnt to ashes in the fire that also engulfed the two adjoining properties, which belonged to Lord Bolingbroke and Lord Perceval. The story of Cantillon's demise might have ended there except for the arrival in the Dutch colony of Surinam,

South America, of a certain Chevalier de Louvigny on December 11, 1734. Rich and well armed, the chevalier attracted the suspicion of Dutch authorities, who attempted to interview him on his arrival in Paramaribo. The chevalier skipped the passport examinations and escaped in a small boat with four black slaves. When the chevalier was later sighted in the jungle, Dutch troops were sent to locate him. However, by the time they arrived the chevalier had once again escaped, though he had left behind some freshly dug earth in his encampment. The Dutch soldiers set to digging and located a large quantity of documents relating to Richard Cantillon, Esquire, of Albemarle Street. The chevalier was never found, leaving us with a further Cantillon mystery. Was the chevalier the French cook, or had Cantillon, despairing of the never-ending civil and criminal litigation against him, arranged his own demise from Europe in the guise of the Chevalier de Louvigny? Although it is highly probable that it was Cantillon's body that was burnt to ashes in Albemarle Street, he may have decided to extend his "unknown" status to South America.

The synopsis of Cantillon's career shows that by the time he came to write his *Essai sur la nature du commerce en général,* sometime between 1728 and 1730, he had considerable experience in the world of banking, finance, and speculation. He was not some ivory-towered theorist but rather a battle-hardened accountant, entrepreneur, banker, and financial trader. He knew the world of money, banking, and financial institutions intimately. He had confidently identified the fault lines of both the Mississippi System and the South Sea scheme, enabling him to make a fortune from both of these stock market bubbles. He had become such an expert on shorting financial markets and currencies that he could have given master classes to many modern exponents of such stratagems.

Essai sur la nature du commerce en général

Publication Background of the Essai

The *Essai* was published posthumously in 1755. The title page states that it was published by Fletcher Gyles in London. This is incorrect, for Fletcher Gyles had died many years before of apoplexy, and the

London imprint was merely a ploy to conceal that it had been published in Paris so as to conform with French censorship laws of the time. The notes of Joseph d'Hémery, who was the supervisor of the book trade (Inspecteur de la Librairie), show that the *Essai* was actually published by the Parisian publisher Guillyn. It soon became known that the author of the *Essai* was Richard Cantillon.

Aside from the published text of the *Essai* (1755), another draft of the *Essai* in French is located at the Bibliothèque Municipale in Rouen.[5] The Rouen manuscript is very inferior to the printed text because it is littered with spelling mistakes and poor punctuation. It contains some differences from the printed text, but none of them could be regarded as substantive.

The Marquis de Mirabeau, author of *L'Ami des hommes* (1756), possessed a further manuscript copy of Cantillon's *Essai*. It appears that he intended to plagiarize and publish the *Essai* under his own name but was prevented from doing so by the publication of the *Essai* in 1755. Mirabeau's selective extraction of large parts of Cantillon's work may be seen in two manuscripts in the Archives Nationales in Paris.[6]

The title page of Cantillon's *Essai* (1755) also states that it has been translated from English. What can be said about the assertion that it was translated from English into French? A growing body of evidence shows that a number of different drafts existed of the English manuscript of the *Essai*. It is already known that Malachy Postlethwayt, a British merchant, had a draft manuscript of Cantillon's *Essai* that he used extensively in two sizable folio volumes titled *The Universal Dictionary of Trade and Commerce* (1751–55). Richard Cantillon's cousin Philip Cantillon also had a manuscript copy, significant parts of which he incorporated into *The Analysis of Trade, Commerce, Coin, Bullion, Bank and Foreign Exchanges . . . Taken chiefly from a ms. of a very ingenious gentleman deceas'd and adapted to the present situation of our trade*

---

5. Cantillon 1979.

6. Details on these manuscripts can be found in Louis Salleron's "Note Liminaire" (Introductory Note) in both the Institut National d'Études Démographiques edition of Cantillon's *Essai* (1952; revised edition 1997, lxv–lxxii) and in the edition edited by Tsuda (1979, 405–10).

and commerce (1759). The "deceas'd gentleman" mentioned in the running title is Richard Cantillon.

Postlethwayt undertook a massive task in producing the *Dictionary*. He publicized his intention of writing this work in a prospectus, *A Dissertation on the Plan, Use, and Importance of the Universal Dictionary of Trade and Commerce* (1749). Hayek showed that Postlethwayt had already started to plagiarize Cantillon in this prospectus.[7] Starting in November 1751 the *Dictionary*, published on a weekly basis in sections, would ultimately comprise 1,017 folio pages in volume 1 and 856 folio pages in volume 2. It was completed in November 1755. This meant that a great part of it had been published prior to the publication of Cantillon's *Essai* in 1755. The *Dictionary* contains lengthy extracts from Cantillon's *Essai*, incorporated by Postlethwayt with no acknowledgment to Richard Cantillon. Furthermore, the quality of the English suggests that these extracts emanate from an English draft or drafts, written by Richard Cantillon, rather than the subsequent French draft that was published as the *Essai* (1755).

Richard van den Berg, working on the texts of both Postlethwayt and Philip Cantillon, has recently been able to show how the English extracts of Cantillon's work derive from a similar-style English text that was the basis for the respective drafts of Postlethwayt and Philip Cantillon.[8] Van den Berg's work appears to confirm that (1) although published in French, the *Essai* was originally composed in English, and (2) the original English draft or drafts of the *Essai* were longer than the published French version.

The existence of Postlethwayt's and Philip Cantillon's English drafts of the *Essai*, as presented in their respective books, makes it more reasonable to concur with Mirabeau's statement that Cantillon translated the *Essai* himself:

> Although he knew our language perfectly, something that may be really seen by a translation that incorporates so many different turns of words

7. Hayek 1985, 234.
8. See van den Berg 2012, 868–907.

and expressions, he was less attentive to the dictation of it than he would have been had he known what is happening to it today.[9]

The fact that both Malachy Postlethwayt and Philip Cantillon had English versions of the *Essai* raises the hope that someday a complete English draft may be found. Who knows whether such a document might also incorporate the elusive missing supplement that Cantillon alludes to a number of times in book 1 of the *Essai*? This supplement was apparently meant to provide statistical evidence to back up some of Cantillon's textual assertions.

The Need for a New Translation[10]

In 1931 Henry Higgs produced a hybrid translation of the *Essai*. In an effort to approximate a contemporaneous translation, Higgs incorporated considerable sections of the *Essai* as found in Postlethwayt's *Universal Dictionary of Trade and Commerce*.[11] Successive generations of economists have used this translation, which has been most useful in showing English readers the originality of Cantillon's intellectual achievement. However, there are problems with Higgs's translation that warrant a new translation.

First, there is no clear delineation between Higgs's translation and his use of Postlethwayt's English extracts of the *Essai*. This makes the overall published text somewhat discontinuous because readers are unsure whether they are reading Higgs's twentieth-century translation or extracts from Postlethwayt's plagiarized passages as found in *The Universal Dictionary of Trade and Commerce*.

Second, Higgs's translation from French into English is excessively

9. See Mirabeau 1753–56. It is difficult to specify a year for manuscript 780 as it is undated. Takumi Tsuda has written that Mirabeau started the manuscript in 1753 and finished it in 1756 (see Cantillon 1979, 403–38).

10. I wish to thank Professor Richard Whatmore and Mr. Charles Ballarin for their reading of the translation, along with their suggestions, which were most useful. Of course, the usual caveat relating to the translator's ultimate responsibility for the text applies.

11. See Cantillon 1931, appendix A, 390.

literal at times. Frequently when translating French sentences, it is necessary to go to the end of the sentence to discover the main clause, which should be at the start of the English translation. In many cases Higgs did not do this.

Third, many key words figuring in the English translation need greater care when translated from the French. To show the nature of this issue, consider three words in particular: *fonds, entrepreneur,* and *consommation.* Higgs translated *fond* and *fonds* as "capital" when they should have been translated as "money," "funds," or even "financial capital."[12] I believe Higgs is wrong to introduce "capital" as the translation of *fond* or *fonds.* By doing so he creates the impression that Cantillon had a clear understanding of the concept of capital. Further, I do not believe that he should have translated *avances* as "capital."[13]

Cantillon actually used the term *capital* and its plural, *les capitaux,* at times, but it is clear that he meant financial capital in these instances.[14]

The second key word that needs discussion in any new translation is *entrepreneur.* Higgs usually translated this in the way it would have been translated in the eighteenth century: "undertaker." Such a translation presents problems for modern students who would not associate an undertaker with the dynamic persona of the modern entrepreneur. Reading the eighteenth-century French, the term corresponds to our modern understanding of the term "entrepreneur." This makes it easy to leave the word as "entrepreneur" in the English translation.

The third example of a key word whose translation is problematic is that of Higgs's conversion of *consommation* into "demand" rather than "consumption."[15] Cantillon used the term *demande* on a number of occasions to signify demand.[16] He had a very good understanding of market forces and the role of demand in the market, as shown by his analysis of the hypothetical pea market in Paris.[17] However, I believe

12. Ibid., 200.
13. Ibid., 299.
14. Ibid., 269, 271, 273, 349, 420, 421.
15. Ibid., 48, 50, 63, 84, 129.
16. Ibid., 157, 158, 216, 362, 366, 383.
17. Ibid., 158.

that translating *consommation* into "demand" puts words into Cantillon's mouth that he did not intend.

There have been further, more recent editions of the *Essai* in both French and English. In 1952 the Institut National d'Études Démographiques republished the original 1755 text of the *Essai* along with commentaries by Anita Fage, Amintore Fanfani, Alfred Sauvy, Louis Salleron, and Joseph J. Spengler. This work was republished with further commentaries by Eric Brian, Antoin E. Murphy, and Christine Théré in 1997.

More recently Chantal Saucier translated and Mark Thornton edited the *Essai* under the strange title *An Essay on Economic Theory* (2010). For this edition, the bracketed page numbers throughout the text refer to the original pagination of the first French edition published in 1755.

The Influence of the Essai

The first edition of the *Essai* was published in 1755. It was quickly followed by a second edition with the same false imprint of Fletcher Gyles in 1756. It also appeared in volume 3 of a collection of works edited by Eléazar Mauvillon under the title *Discours Politiques,* which was published in 1756 and republished in 1769. Four French publications of the *Essai* in the space of fourteen years suggests a significant French interest in the *Essai*. P. M. Scottoni translated it into Italian: *Saggio sulla natura del commercio in generale.* This translation was published in 1767 in Venice.

The *Essai* was published alongside many other works on trade (*le commerce*) that emanated from a pre-Physiocratic group led by Vincent de Gournay in France of the 1750s. Cantillon's work helped inspire this group, which espoused a new *laissez-faire, laissez-passer* approach. On the death of Gournay in 1759, the leadership of the group known as *les économistes* effectively passed to François Quesnay. Quesnay produced the first diagrammatic explanation of the macroeconomy in the *Tableau économique* (1758/59).[18] This work was heavily influenced by Cantillon's detailed account of the circular flow of income process.

18. See Quesnay 1972, 2005.

Quesnay greatly advanced Cantillon's contribution to the macroeconomic debate by showing the potential for the economy to achieve economic growth, countering the mercantilistic approach that envisaged the economic process as a zero-sum game.

Cantillon's work influenced not only the French economists but also Adam Smith. Smith's key chapter on the role of the market in allocating resources is found in book 1, chapter 7, of *An Inquiry into the Nature and Causes of the Wealth of Nations* (1776). In this chapter, titled "Of the Natural and Market Price of Commodities," Smith distinguishes between the market price and the natural price to show how resources would be moved into or out of specific markets accordingly as these prices diverge. Smith's analysis borrows from Cantillon's distinction between market price and intrinsic value, and a great part of his discussion represents a paraphrase of Cantillon's earlier analysis.

Cantillon's influence on the pre-Physiocrats, the Physiocrats, and Adam Smith was considerable. Despite this, the *Essai* lay dormant for much of the nineteenth century until it was once again brought to the attention of economists by Stanley Jevons in an article titled "Richard Cantillon and the Nationality of Political Economy," first published in *Contemporary Review* in January 1881 and republished in the Higgs edition of Cantillon's *Essai* (1931). Jevons concluded that the *Essai* represented "the veritable cradle of Political Economy."[19] Henry Higgs, inspired by his former lecturer, Professor Henry Foxwell, continued the movement to reappraise Cantillon's book when providing the first English translation of the *Essai,* along with an introduction, in the Royal Economics Society/Macmillan edition of the *Essai* in 1931. In his introduction Higgs expressed the following view:

> After reading well over a thousand economic writings of earlier date than 1734 I would put Cantillon's analysis of the circulation of wealth, trite as it may now appear, on the same level of priority as Harvey's study of the circulation of the blood.[20]

19. See Cantillon 1931, 359.
20. Ibid., 388.

The *Essai* is remarkable on many fronts, and economists have found in it a wide range of issues that are of considerable appeal; see such works as Bordo (1983), Brewer (1992), Hayek (1936), Murphy (1986, 2009), and Spengler (1954a, 1954b) as well as the contributors to the Institut National d'Études Démographiques edition of Cantillon's *Essai* (1997). This is not the place to analyze Cantillon's economics. It is hoped that readers of this translation may be able to discover further insights into the remarkable ideas of this *inconnu,* who had such a significant and lasting influence on the economic ideas of the eighteenth century.

ANTOIN E. MURPHY
Fellow Emeritus
Trinity College Dublin

REFERENCES

Baker, C. H. Collins, and Muriel Baker. 1949. *The Life and Circumstances of James Brydges, First Duke of Chandos, Patron of the Liberal Arts.* Oxford: Clarendon Press.

Bordo, Michael. 1983. "Some Aspects of the Monetary Economics of Richard Cantillon." *Journal of Monetary Economics* 12, no. 2: 235–58.

Brewer, Anthony. 1992. *Richard Cantillon: Pioneer of Economic Theory.* London and New York: Routledge.

Cantillon, Richard. 1931. *Essai sur la nature du commerce en général.* Edited and translated by Henry Higgs for the Royal Economic Society. London: Macmillan & Co.

———. 1979. *Essay de la nature du commerce en général.* Edited by Takumi Tsuda. Tokyo: Kinokuniya.

———. 1997. *Essai sur la nature du commerce en général.* Paris: Institut National d'Études Démographiques.

———. 2010. *An Essay on Economic Theory.* Translated by Chantal Saucier and edited by Mark Thornton. Auburn, Ala.: Ludwig Von Mises Institute.

Du Hautchamp, Barthélemy Marmont. 1743. *Histoire générale et particulière du Visa.* 2 vols. The Hague.

Hayek, Friedrich von. 1936. "Richard Cantillon: Sa vie, son oeuvre." *Revue des sciences économiques* 10 (April, June, October).

———. 1985. "Richard Cantillon." *Journal of Libertarian Studies* 7, no. 2: 217–47. [Translation of Hayek's introduction to the German edition of the *Essay*.]

Mirabeau, Victor Riqueti de. 1753–56. *Mémoire sur la population.* Ms. 780. Paris: Archives Nationales.

Murphy, Antoin E. 1986. *Richard Cantillon: Entrepreneur and Economist.* Oxford: Clarendon Press; New York: Oxford University Press.

———. 1997. *John Law: Economic Theorist and Policy-Maker.* Oxford: Clarendon Press; New York: Oxford University Press.

———. 2009. *The Genesis of Macroeconomics: New Ideas from Sir William Petty to Henry Thornton.* Oxford and New York: Oxford University Press.

Postlethwayt, Malachy. 1751–55. *The Universal Dictionary of Trade and Commerce.* London.

Quesnay, François. 1972. *Quesnay's Tableau économique.* Edited by Marguerite Kuczynski and Ronald L. Meek. London: Macmillan; New York: A. M. Kelley for the Royal Economic Society and the American Economic Association.

———. 2005. *Oeuvres économiques complètes et autres textes.* Edited by Christine Théré, Loic Charles, and Jean-Claude Perrot. Paris: Institut National d'Études Démographiques.

Smith, Adam. 1776. *An Inquiry into the Nature and Causes of the Wealth of Nations.* London.

Spengler, Joseph. 1954a. "Richard Cantillon: First of the Moderns. I." *Journal of Political Economy* 62 (August): 281–95.

———. 1954b. "Richard Cantillon: First of the Moderns. II." *Journal of Political Economy* 62 (October): 406–24.

van den Berg, Richard. 2012. "'Something Wonderful and Incomprehensible in Their Oeconomy': The English Versions of Richard Cantillon's *Essay on the Nature of Trade in General.*" *European Journal of the History of Economic Thought* 19, (December): 868–907.

Part I

I

Of wealth

Land is the source or the matter from which wealth is derived; labor is the form that produces it, and wealth in itself is nothing other [2] than food, commodities, and the comforts of life.

Land produces grasslands, roots, cereals, linen, cotton, hemp, many types of shrubs, and timbers that provide fruits, bark, and different types of leaves such as those of the mulberry for silkworms; it produces mines and minerals. Labor gives the form of wealth to all of this.

The rivers and seas provide fish for man's food and many other things for his enjoyment. But these seas and rivers are common to all or belong to adjacent lands, and man's labor extracts fish and other advantages from them. [3]

2

Of human societies

Irrespective of the way human society is constituted, the ownership of habitable land will nevertheless necessarily belong to a small number of people.

It is necessary for the leader or king in nomadic societies, such as those of the Tartar hordes and Indian tribes, who travel with their animals and families from one place to another, to apportion the quarters and boundaries for each head of family and for everyone around the camp. Otherwise there would always be disputes concerning the quarters or living conveniences, woods, pastures, water, and so forth, but when the [4] quarters and boundaries of each person are determined, this will be as good as the ownership of land for the duration of their stay in that place.

In more settled societies, if a prince at the head of an army has conquered a country, he will distribute the lands to his officers or favorites according to their merit or his pleasure (this was originally the case in France); he will establish laws to keep the estates for them and their descendants; or, alternatively, he (the prince) will reserve for himself the ownership of the land and will entrust his officers or favorites with the task of exploiting their value; or he will concede it to them on condition of their paying an annual quit rent or rent; or he will make a grant to them while reserving the right to tax them annually according to his own requirements. In all such cases, these officers or favorites will constitute only a small part of the whole population whether they are absolute owners, or [5] dependents, or stewards, or bailiffs of the produce of the land.

Now the land, even if distributed in equal portions to all of the inhabitants by the prince, will still end up in the hands of few. One inhabitant may have several children and thus will be unable to leave each of them an equal portion of the land similar to his own; another may die childless and leave his portion to someone who already has a portion of his own, rather than to someone who has none; a third may be lazy, prodigal, or infirm and will be obliged to sell his portion to someone else, who, through his frugality and industry, will continually increase his lands by buying more land, which he will then develop through the work of those who, [6] being landless, will be obliged to offer their labor in order to subsist.

When Rome was first settled, each inhabitant was given two acres[1] of land; nevertheless, this did not prevent as great an inequality soon afterward in the ownership of estates as that seen today across all the states of Europe. A small number of people ultimately owned the land.

Supposing, then, that the lands of a new state belong to a small number of people, each owner will either manage the lands himself or will entrust them to one or more farmers; in such an economy, it is indispensable that the farmers and the laborers cover the costs of their subsistence [7] whether it is managed by the owner himself or by the

1. Abel Boyer, *Dictionnaire Royale François-Anglois et Anglois-François* (Amsterdam, 1727), defines a *journal ou journau* as an acre of land (n.p.). —AEM

farmer. The landlord receives the surplus product of the land; he is obliged to pay part of it to the prince or the state, or, alternatively, the farmer will pay [this tax] directly to the prince and deduct it from that paid to the owner.

With regard to the use of the land, it is necessary to employ part of it for the upkeep and maintenance of those who work and make it productive; the rest is principally dependent on the preferences and lifestyle of the prince, the lords, and the owner; if they like drinking, the vines will need to be cultivated; if they like silks, mulberry trees need to be planted and silkworms raised; furthermore, a proportionate part of the land needs to be employed for the maintenance [8] of those required to carry out this work; if they like horses, pastures will be required, and so on.

However, in the absence of land ownership, it would be difficult to conceive how a society of men could be formed; for example, we see with commons that the number of animals that each inhabitant may send there is restricted; and, if lands were given to the first occupier in a new conquest or on the discovery of a country, it is always necessary to be able to refer to an ownership rule in order for a society to be established, whether this rule is decided by force or by civil government. [9]

3 *Of villages*

Irrespective of the type of land cultivation, whether it is in pasture, wheat, or vineyards, it is always necessary for the farmers or laborers who work on them to live nearby; otherwise too much of the day would be taken up by time spent in going to the fields and returning to their houses. Hence the need for villages to be spread across all the countryside and cultivated lands, where there must also be enough farriers and wheelwrights for the tools, plows, and carts that are necessary, especially when the village is distant from the towns and cities. The size of a village in terms of [10] inhabitants dependent upon the land is naturally proportioned to the number of people that the land requires for its cultivation, as well as the number of the craftsmen who find sufficient employment providing services for the farmers and laborers. But these craftsmen are not quite as necessary in the neighborhood of cities, where laborers can go without wasting too much time.

If one or more of the village's landlords take up residence there, the number of inhabitants will be greater in proportion to the number of servants and craftsmen that they will attract and in proportion to the inns that will be established for the benefit of the servants and workers who are maintained by these landlords.

If, as in sandy areas [11] and moorlands, the quality of the land is sufficient only to feed flocks of sheep, villages will be rarer and smaller because the land requires only a small number of shepherds.

If the land is on sandy soil limited to afforestation, where there is no grass for animals, and if it is distant from cities and rivers, which makes these forests unfit for human exploitation, such forests as are sometimes seen in Germany, houses and villages will be present only to the extent necessary for the seasonal collection of acorns and the feeding of pigs; but if the land is completely barren, there will be no inhabitants or villages. [12]

4 *Of market towns*

There are some villages where markets have been established due to the interest of a landlord or a royal courtier. These markets, held once or twice a week, encourage several small entrepreneurs and merchants to establish themselves there, where they can purchase commodities in the market brought from the local villages, in order to transport and sell them in the cities. In exchange for these commodities they purchase iron, salt, sugar, and other goods in the cities and sell them during market days to the villages' inhabitants. Many craftsmen, such as locksmiths, cabinetmakers, [13] and others, missing from the original community, establish themselves for the benefit of the villagers, a development that eventually creates towns. It is easier and more natural for the villagers to buy and sell their commodities on market days at a market town situated at the center of the surrounding villages than to see the merchants and entrepreneurs bring these commodities to the villages to exchange them for those that are locally produced. (1) Merchants' travel between villages would unnecessarily increase the costs of transport. (2) These merchants would possibly have to travel to many villages to search for the quality and quantity of the commodities that they wished to purchase. (3) Often, when the merchants arrived, the villagers [14] would be in the fields having nothing ready or presentable to display because they were unable to judge the type of commodities that were required. (4) It would be almost impossible, in the villages, to agree on commodity prices between the merchants and the villagers. The merchant could refuse the village price for the commodity in expectation that he could find it at a better price in another village, and the villagers could refuse the merchant's price for a commodity in expectation that another merchant would come and take it on better terms.

All these difficulties are avoided when the villagers come to town on market days to sell their commodities and to buy [15] what they need. Prices are fixed by the proportion of commodities presented for sale and by the money offered to purchase them; this takes place in the same spot and is observed by the villagers from different villages and the town's merchants and entrepreneurs. When the prices have been determined between a few, the rest follow without difficulty, and it is thereby possible to establish the market price on that day. The peasant then returns to his village and resumes his work.

The size of the market town is naturally proportioned to the number of farmers and laborers that are needed to cultivate the lands dependent on it and to the number of craftsmen and small merchants that the villages surrounding the town employ, as well as their assistants and horses, and finally to the number of people [16] who make a living from the resident landlords.

When the villages surrounding the market town (i.e., those whose inhabitants usually bring their produce to this town's market) are important and have many products, then the market town will become proportionately larger and more significant; but when the surrounding villages produce little, the town is also poor and insignificant.

5   *Of cities*

The owners of small estates normally live in towns and villages near their land and their farmers. The transportation of the commodities originating from them to distant towns [17] would deprive them of the means of living comfortably in these towns. But the owners of many large estates have the means of living far from their land so as to enjoy the good company of other owners of estates and nobles of a similar condition.

A place will become a city if a noble or prince who has been granted sizable amounts of land during the conquest or discovery of a country situates his residence in an agreeable area there, and if many other noblemen come and reside alongside him so as to be together often and to enjoy good company. Great houses will be built there as the residences of the nobility in question; many others will be built there for merchants, craftsmen, and people of many different professions attracted to this place [18] by the presence of the nobility. Butchers, bakers, brewers, wine merchants, and manufacturers of all kinds will be required to service these nobles. These entrepreneurs will build houses in the area in question or will rent houses built by other entrepreneurs. The detailed calculations that I made in the supplement[2] of this essay show how the great nobleman through his expenditure on his household, his lifestyle, and his servants maintains a wide range of merchants and craftsmen.

2. The supplement is missing. —AEM

As all these craftsmen and entrepreneurs provide services to one another as well as to their rightful lord, no one perceives that the maintenance of everyone is ultimately the burden of the nobles and landlords, any more [19] than that all the small houses in a city, such as have been described here, are dependent on and live off the expenditure of the great houses. It will, however, be shown in what follows that all the orders and inhabitants of a state subsist at the expense of landlords. The city in question will expand further if the king or the government establishes law courts to which the inhabitants of the towns and the villages of the province may turn in time of need. An increase of all types of entrepreneurs and artisans will be necessary for the upkeep of the legal officials and lawyers.

If additional craft goods and manufactures are created over and above those amounts required domestically, so as to be exported and sold abroad, the city will be sizable in terms of workers and craftsmen living [20] at the expense of the foreigner.

But, leaving aside these ideas so as not to complicate our subject, it may be said that the assembly of several rich landlords, who live together in the same place, is sufficient to create what is called a city and that many European cities situated inland owe the number of their inhabitants to this type of gathering; in which case the size of a city is naturally proportioned to the number of landlords who live there, or, more particularly, to their lands' produce, net of the costs of transport for those whose lands are situated farther afield, and the amount that they are obliged to furnish to the king or the state, which is usually to be consumed in the capital city. [21]

6 Of capital cities

A capital city is established in the same way as a provincial city, with the difference that the largest landlords in the state reside there, the king or the supreme government lives there and spends the state's revenues there, the courts of final appeal are based there, it is the center of fashion that the provinces take as their model, and it is the place where the landlords who live in the provinces come and stay from time to time and to which they send their children to be further educated. Thus all the lands [22] of the state contribute more or less to the maintenance of the capital's inhabitants.

If a sovereign leaves a city to establish his residence in another place, the nobility is sure to follow suit and live with him in the new city, which will grow in importance at the expense of the former. A recent example of this was St. Petersburg at the expense of Moscow, and one has seen many old cities that were sizable collapse in decay while others have been reborn from their ashes. To facilitate transport, large cities have usually been built beside the sea or on rivers because the cost of carriage by water of commodities and produce necessary for the inhabitants' subsistence and comfort is far cheaper [23] than when carried out by carriages and transport on land.

7   *The work of a laborer is worth less than that of a craftsman*

A laborer's son, at the age of seven or twelve years, starts to help his father either by minding flocks, or digging earth, or carrying out other rural works that require neither art nor skill.

If the father makes him learn a trade, he loses because of his absence during the time of his apprenticeship, and into the bargain is obliged to pay for several years' worth of his upkeep and apprenticeship's expenses. The son, whose work brings no benefit [24] except at the end of a certain number of years, lives at the expense of his father. Because a man's [working] life is calculated at no more than ten or twelve years, and as many of these are lost learning a craft—in England most apprenticeships are for seven years—a laborer would have no reason to have his son apprenticed unless craftsmen earn more than laborers.

Those who employ artisans or craftsmen, therefore, must necessarily pay more for their work than for that of a laborer or a mason's assistant, and this work will be necessarily expensive in proportion to the amount of time lost in the apprenticeship and the expense and risks involved in becoming a proficient craftsman.

Craftsmen themselves will not have all their children apprenticed; many of them [25] would not find enough work because there would be an excess of them relative to the needs of a city or a state. This work, however, is always naturally more expensive than that of the laborers.

8

Some craftsmen earn more and others less according to different cases and circumstances

If there are two tailors who make all the clothes of a village, one may have more customers than the other either because of his method of attracting business, or because his work is superior or more durable than the other, or because he can better follow the fashion through the cut of his clothes.

If one of them dies, the other, finding himself with a great deal more work, will be able to raise [26] his prices and give preference to certain customers, up to the point where the villagers will find it advantageous, even losing the time in coming and going, to have their clothes made in another village, town, or city, or until that time when another tailor arrives to live in their village and share the work.

The crafts that should naturally be the best paid are those that require the longest time to perfect or require more skill and industry. A skilled cabinetmaker should be paid a better price for his work than an ordinary carpenter, as also a good watchmaker more than a farrier.

Risky and dangerous arts and crafts such as those of founders, sailors, silver miners, and the like [27] must be paid in proportion to the risks they undertake. When into the bargain, over and above the dangers, skill is required, they should be paid even more; such are the cases of pilots, divers, engineers, and so on. Labor is even more expensive when skill and confidence are required, such as in the cases of jewelers, bookkeepers, cashiers, and others.

It may be easily shown by these examples and a hundred others drawn from everyday life that the different prices paid for daily work result from natural and sensible reasons. [28]

9 The number of laborers, craftsmen, and others who work in a state is naturally proportioned to the need for them

If all of a village's laborers raise many sons for the same work, there will be too many of them to cultivate the village's lands, and it will be necessary for these surplus adults to go elsewhere to earn their living, as is normally the case for those who live in the cities. As those who remain alongside their fathers will not find sufficient employment, they will live in considerable poverty and will not marry, because they lack the means to raise children, or, if they do marry, [29] the children born to them will perish in misery shortly afterward with their parents, as we see every day in France.

Therefore the population of the village will not expand in a thousand years if it continues to follow the same conditions of work and derives its subsistence by cultivating the same portion of land.

It is true that the village's women and daughters, when not working in the fields, can occupy themselves through spinning, knitting, and other works that can be sold in the towns. But this rarely suffices to raise the surplus children, who must leave the village to seek their fortune elsewhere.

One can reason in the same way about the village's craftsmen. If a single tailor makes all the clothes there, and raises three [30] sons in the same craft, it will be necessary for two of them to seek their living elsewhere, as there will be work only for the son who succeeds him. If the other sons do not find work in the neighboring town, they will have to travel farther, or change their job by becoming lackeys, soldiers, sailors, or the like in order to make a living.

It is easy to reason, in the same way, that laborers, craftsmen, and others who make their living by working must be proportionate in number to the employment and need for them in the market towns and cities.

But if a fifth tailor arrives when four tailors suffice to produce all the town's clothes, he may attract some employment at the expense of the other four in such a way that, when the work [31] is carried out by the five tailors, none of them will have enough work and each will thrive less.

When too many laborers and craftsmen share work, it often happens that there is insufficient employment for them. Frequently, they may also be deprived of work by accidents and by changes in patterns of consumption. It can also happen that, following certain cases and changes, they have too much work. Whatever the case, when they are unemployed they will leave the villages, towns, or cities where they live, in such numbers that those who remain will always be in proportion to the employment that suffices for their subsistence; and when a continuous increase in work occurs there will be opportunities, [32] and many others will come to contribute to the work.

It is easy to see from these examples that English charity schools and French schemes to increase the number of craftsmen are both pointless. It would be useless for the king of France to send a hundred thousand of his subjects to learn seafaring in Holland if, on their return, more ships were not sent to sea than formerly. Yet it is true that it would be enormously advantageous for a state to educate its subjects to manufacture those goods that are customarily imported from abroad, along with all the other articles that are bought there. But currently I am considering only a state with reference to itself.

Since the craftsmen earn more than the laborers, they are in a better position than the latter to train [33] their children in crafts, and there will always be enough craftsmen in a state when there is enough work for their constant employment.

The price and intrinsic value of a thing in general is the amount of land and labor required to produce it

One acre of land produces more wheat, or feeds more sheep, than another acre. As already explained, a man's work is more expensive than that of another according to his skill and the circumstances of the time. If two acres of land are similarly fertile and are worked in the same manner, one acre will maintain as many sheep and will produce the same quantity of wool as [34] the other, and the wool produced by one will sell at the same price as that produced by the other.

If wool drawn from one acre is made into a suit of coarse cloth, and wool from the other acre made into a suit of fine cloth, the latter suit, requiring a greater amount of work, which is dearer than that of the former, will sometimes be up to ten times as expensive, even though both suits contain the same quantity and quality of wool. The quantity of the earth's produce, and both the quantity and quality of the labor, will necessarily enter into the price.

It may be seen in a comparison of different work processes in the supplement that a pound of flax worked into fine Brussels lace requires the work of fourteen people over a year, or the work of one person over [35] fourteen years. It may also be seen that the price for this lace suffices to pay for the upkeep of a person for fourteen years and also to pay for all the profits of the entrepreneurs and merchants involved.

The fine steel spring that regulates an English watch normally sells at a price that makes the proportion of material to labor, or the steel to the spring, at one to one [million],[3] in such a way that the labor here

3. The missing figure here is a printer's or transcriber's error. The French manuscripts of the *Essai,* located in the Archives Nationales and the Bibliothèque Municipale in Rouen, provide a figure of "un à 1538460." Postlethwayt, who plagiarized a sizable section of Cantillon's *Essai* and may possibly have been working

constitutes almost entirely the value of this spring. See the calculation in the supplement.

On the other hand, the price of hay in a field delivered on the spot, or a wood to be cut down, is determined by its quality, or by the produce of [36] the earth, according to its fertility.

As it is an immense river, and does not dry out, a pitcher of Seine water costs nothing. But in the streets of Paris a penny is given for it, the price or the measure of the labor of the water carrier.

By this evidence and these examples, I believe that it may be understood that the price, or the intrinsic value, of a thing is the measure of the quantity of land and of labor that enters into its production, due regard being given to the fertility or produce of the land and to the quality of the labor involved.

But it often arises that many things that actually have this intrinsic value do not sell in the market according to this value; that will depend on people's moods and whims and on their consumption.

[37] If a lord cuts drains and builds terraces in his garden, their intrinsic value will be proportionate to the land and labor undertaken; but the price in reality will not always follow this proportion. If he offers to sell this garden, it could happen that no one will be willing to give him even half the cost of his expenses. But it could also happen that if several people want it, they could offer him double the intrinsic value, that is, twice the value of the land and the expenses he incurred.

If the farmers in a state sow more wheat than usual, that is, a great deal more than is needed for annual consumption, the intrinsic and real value of the wheat will correspond to the land and labor used in its

---

on an even more extended manuscript, has one to one million; see Malachy Postlethwayt (1755), *The Universal Dictionary of Trade and Commerce*, vol. 2, p. 1. In another of his works, *Great Britain's True System* (1757), Postlethwayt produced the figure found in the French manuscripts of 1 to 1,538,460. It would appear most likely that the missing figure in the French text as translated above should be 1,538,460. I am indebted to Richard van den Berg for this information; see Richard van den Berg, "'Something Wonderful and Incomprehensible in Their Oeconomy': The English Versions of Richard Cantillon's *Essay on the Nature of Trade in General*," *European Journal of the History of Economic Thought* 19 (December 2012): 868–907. —AEM

production. But, as there is too great [38] an abundance of it, and more sellers than buyers, the market price of the wheat will necessarily fall below the price or intrinsic value. If, on the other hand, the farmers sow less wheat than is needed for consumption, there will be more buyers than sellers, and the price of wheat in the market will rise above its intrinsic value.

The intrinsic value of things is not subject to change, but in a state, the impossibility of proportioning the production of merchandise and commodities to their consumption causes daily variations and a continual ebb and flow of market prices. In well-regulated societies, however, the market prices of commodities and merchandise whose consumption is sufficiently constant and uniform do not vary [39] much from the intrinsic value. Except in years of dearth or overabundance, the city's magistrates are always in a position to fix the market prices of many things, such as bread and meat, without any cause for complaints.

Land is the matter, and labor is the form, of all types of commodities and merchandise; and as those who work must necessarily subsist on the produce of the land, it appears that it should be possible to find a relation between the value of labor and that of the land's produce. This will be the subject of the following chapter. [40]

II Of the par or relation between the value of the land and the value of labor

It does not appear that Providence has given the right of land ownership to one man rather than to another. The oldest titles are founded on violence and on conquest. Today the lands of Mexico belong to the Spanish and those of Jerusalem to the Turks. But we have already seen that, irrespective of the manner of the acquisition and the possession of lands, they always devolve on a small number of people out of the total population.

If the owner of a great estate decides to manage [41] it himself, he will employ either slaves or free people to work it. If he employs many slaves on it, he must have supervisors to make them work. He also needs craftsmen slaves to produce the commodities and comforts of life for himself and for those whom he employs. He will also need to teach crafts to others to ensure the continuity of work.

In this economy it is necessary for him to give his slave laborers a simple subsistence along with the means for raising their children. He needs to give their supervisors advantages in proportion to the authority and confidence that they possess. He needs to provide maintenance, without any recompense, for the slaves whom he is having instructed in crafts during their apprenticeships. He needs to give working craftsmen [42] slaves and their supervisors, who have to have a competent understanding of the crafts, a proportionately greater subsistence than he gives to the slave laborers, etc., because the loss of a craftsman would be far greater than that of a laborer, and greater care must be taken of him, considering the costs of teaching someone to replace him.

On this assumption, the labor of the lowliest adult slave corresponds to and is worth at least the quantity of land that the owner is obliged to use to feed and provide him with the necessary commodities, and also twice the quantity of land required to raise a child until laboring age, given that, according to the calculations and observations of the renowned [43] Doctor Halley, half the children who are born die before the age of seventeen years. Thus, it is necessary to raise two children in order to have one of working age, and it appears that even this calculation is not sufficient to ensure the continuity of work, because adult men die at all ages.

It is true that the mortality rate of half of the children who are born and die before the age of seventeen years is a great deal higher in the first rather than the later years of their lives, since a good third of those who are born die in their first year. This outcome appears to reduce the cost of rearing a child until laboring age. But, as mothers lose a great deal of time in caring for their children during their illnesses and early childhood, and girls, even when adults, do not provide as much work as males and scarcely earn enough to subsist, [44] it appears that, in order to raise one of two children to adolescence or the age of working, it is necessary to use as much of the land's produce as is needed for the subsistence of an adult slave *whether the owner raises the children himself or has them raised in his house, or whether the slave father raises them in a separate house or hamlet. Thus I conclude that the daily labor of the slave of the meanest condition corresponds in value to double the land's produce necessary to maintain him, whether the owner gives it to him for his own and his family's subsistence* or whether he provides it for him and his family in his own house. In this discussion, which does not produce an exact calculation and where precision is not really necessary, it is sufficient not to stray too far from the truth.

If the owner employs [45] vassals or free peasants for his work, he will probably maintain them better than slaves, depending on local practice. But again this supposes that the work of a free laborer must correspond in value to double the land's produce necessary for his maintenance. But it will always be more advantageous for the owner to keep slaves rather than free peasants, given that when he has raised too many of the former for work he will be able, as is the case with cattle, to sell the excess, thereby producing a price proportionate to the expenditure involved in raising them to adolescence or the age of work, except for those cases involving old age and illness.

The labor of craftsmen slaves can also be estimated at double the produce of the land that they consume, [46] that of the labor supervisors similarly according to the favors and advantages given to them over and above those working under them.

If the laborers or craftsmen are married, with their double portion at their disposal, they use one part for their own upkeep and the other to raise their children. If they are bachelors they will put aside a small part of their double portion to enable them to marry and have a small sum available for the household. Most of them will, however, use up their double portion for their own requirements.

A married peasant, for example, will be happy to live off bread, cheese, vegetables, and the like and will rarely eat meat, will drink little wine or beer, and will always have old and worn [47] clothes, which he will wear as long as possible. He will employ the surplus of his double portion for the maintenance and upkeep of his children. By way of contrast, the bachelor peasant, eating meat as often as possible and buying himself new clothes and so forth, will consequently use up his double portion for his own requirements. Thereby, he will personally consume twice the amount of the land's produce than that of the married peasant.

Here I have not taken into consideration the wife's expenditure, assuming that her work barely suffices for her own upkeep. It may be surmised, when one sees a large family in one of these poor households, that their subsistence is aided by some charitable people, without which both the husband and his wife will need to deprive themselves of part of their necessities [48] in order to ensure the survival of their children.

To better comprehend this, it should be understood that, according to the lowest estimate, a poor peasant may survive on the produce of an acre and a half of land if he eats bread and vegetables, wears hempen garments and clogs, etc. If he can, however, consume wine, meat, woolen clothes, etc., without drunkenness, gluttony, or excesses, he may be able to spend the produce of between four and ten acres of medium-quality land such as is normally found, all things considered, across Europe. In the supplement I have made some calculations to assess the amount of land necessary for one man's annual consumption on his food, clothing, and other necessities of life, [49] bearing in mind the varying European standards of living, where the peasants of different countries are often fed and maintained in a dissimilar manner.

On account of that, I had not determined the corresponding land-to-labor value of the poorest peasant or laborer when I remarked that it was worth twice the amount of land needed to maintain him, because that value varies according to the way of living in different countries. In some parts of the south of France the peasant maintains himself on the produce of one and a half acres of land, while his labor may be estimated as being equal to the produce of three acres. But in the County of Middlesex the peasant normally spends the produce of five to eight acres of land, and thus his labor may be estimated at double this.

In the Iroquois territories, where [50] the natives, living uniquely through hunting, do not till the land, the lowliest hunter may consume the produce of fifty acres of land, since it probably requires that acreage to feed the animals that he annually eats, particularly since these savages leave everything to nature and are not industrious enough to grow grass by clearing some of the forest.

It is therefore possible to value this hunter's labor as equal to the produce of 100 acres of land. In the south of China the land produces rice up to three times per year and each time yields up to 100 times what is sown, arising from the great care that the inhabitants take in agriculture, and because of the fertility of the soil, which never lies fallow. The peasants who are working there are almost naked, [51] living uniquely on rice and drinking only rice water. It appears that one acre maintains more than ten peasants, and therefore it is not astonishing to find such a prodigious number of inhabitants there. In any case these examples show that nature is indifferent as to whether the lands are cultivated in the form of meadow, forest, or grain, or whether they maintain a great or small number of vegetables, animals, or people.

The European farmers appear to correspond to the supervisors of the laboring slaves in other countries, and the master craftsmen who direct several journeymen are similar to the supervisors of the craftsmen slaves.

These master craftsmen know almost exactly how much work a journeyman craftsman can produce daily in each craft [52] and often pay them in proportion to the work that they produce; thus these journeymen toil, unsupervised, as hard as they can for their own advantage.

As European farmers and master craftsmen are all entrepreneurs working at risk, some become rich and earn more than double their subsistence while others are ruined and become bankrupt, as will be explained more particularly later when discussing entrepreneurs. But most of them support themselves and their families on a daily basis, and their work or supervision may be estimated at nearly three times that of the land's produce, which serves for their maintenance.

It is certain that, if these farmers and master craftsmen manage the work of ten laborers or journeymen, they should also be [53] capable of managing the work of twenty, depending on the size of their farms or the number of their customers; this is what makes the value of their work or supervisory labors uncertain.

Through these and other examples, which may be made in a similar manner, it can be seen that the value of daily labor has a relationship with the produce of the land, and that the intrinsic value of a thing may be measured by the quantity of land that is used in its production and by the quantity of labor that enters into it, that is, by the quantity of land whose produce is attributed to those who work on it. As all these lands belong to the prince and to the landlords, all the things that have that intrinsic value have it exclusively at their expense.

Money or coin, which [54] *finds the equivalence of its value in exchange, is the most certain measure to evaluate the par between land and labor and the relationship that one has to the other in different countries, where this par varies according to whether a greater or lesser amount of the land's produce is attributed to those who labor.*

For example, if every day one man earns an ounce of silver by his labor, whereas another earns only half an ounce in the same place, it may be concluded that the first has double the land's produce to spend than the second.

Sir William Petty, in a short manuscript of the year 1685, considers this par, through the equation between land and labor, as the most important consideration in political arithmetic. But the research, which he carried out in passing, is strange and remote [55] from natural laws because he disregarded the causes and principles and considered only the effects, just as has been the case with Locke and Davenant and all the other English authors who have subsequently written something about this after him.

12 All classes and men in the state are maintained or enriched at the expense of the landlords

Only the prince and the landlords live independently; all the other classes and inhabitants are hired or are entrepreneurs. In the next chapter the proof and detail of this will be more particularly developed.

It is evident that if the prince and the land owners [56] closed their lands and refused to allow people to work them, there would be no food or clothing for the state's inhabitants. In consequence, all the state's inhabitants not only live from the produce of the land that is cultivated on behalf of the owners of the land, but live also at the expense of these same owners from whom they derive all that they have.

The farmers usually have two-thirds of the land's produce, one for expenses and the maintenance of their assistants, and the other constituting the profits of their business. From these two-thirds the farmer generally ensures the subsistence of all those who live directly or indirectly in the country, and even ensures the subsistence of several of the city's craftsmen or entrepreneurs because of the goods [57] from the city that are consumed in the country.

The owner normally has a third of the land's produce, and with this third he maintains all of those that he employs in the city, not only craftsmen and others, but also, frequently, the carriers who bring goods from the country to the city.

It may generally be supposed that half of a state's inhabitants subsist and live in the cities and the other half in the country. This being the case, the farmer who has two-thirds or four-sixths of the land's produce gives one-sixth of it directly or indirectly to the urban inhabitants in exchange for the commodities that he takes from them. This, along with the third or two-sixths that the owner spends in the city, makes three-sixths, or half, of the land's produce. [58] This calculation is provided just to give a general idea of the proportion, for the reason that if half of the inhabitants live in the city, urban expenditure will be greater than half the land's produce, given that urban inhabitants live better than those in the country, and as [in the city] they are all craftsmen or the owners' dependents, and consequently better kept than the workers and farmers' dependents [in the country], they spend more of the land's produce.

Whatever be the case, it will always be found, when an inhabitant's means of subsistence are examined and traced back to their source, that they originate from the owner's own land, whether it is the two-thirds of the produce attributed to the farmer or the third that goes to the owner.

If an owner had only the quantity of land that he gives [59] to a single farmer, this farmer would live better than the owner. But the city's lords and the owners of great estates often employ several hundreds of farmers, and constitute only a very small part of a state's population.

It is true that often many entrepreneurs and craftsmen in the big cities live off foreign trade, and consequently at the expense of landlords in foreign countries. To avoid complicating my subject with incidental matter, I am considering solely a state with reference to its own produce and industry.

The land itself belongs to the owners of the land, but this land would be useless if it was not cultivated, and, all other things being equal, the more it is worked, the more it produces. The more these articles are labored upon, all other things [60] being equal, the greater the value they will have once turned into merchandise. This means that the owners need the other inhabitants, just as the latter need the owners. In such an economy, however, it is up to the owners, who have the lands at their disposal and under their control, to give the most advantageous impulse to all things. I will also try to show clearly in the latter part of this essay that all things principally depend on the whims, fashions, and lifestyles of the landlords.

Want and necessity enable farmers to subsist, and also all types of craftsmen, merchants, officers, soldiers, sailors, domestics, and all the [61] other classes who work or are employed in the state. All these working people not only serve the prince and the landlords, but also mutually serve one another in such a way that, because some of them do not work directly for the landlords, it is not apparent that they draw their livelihoods from the land, and live at the expense of the latter. Actors, painters, musicians, and the like, working in nonessential professions and whose numbers are always small relative to the rest of the population, are maintained in a state only for pleasure or ornament. [62]

13

The circulation and exchange of goods, as well as the production of goods and of merchandise, are carried out in Europe by entrepreneurs in conditions of risk

The farmer is an entrepreneur who, without any certainty about what advantages he will derive from the enterprise, promises to pay the owner a fixed sum of money for his farm or land—which is normally assumed to be equal in value to a third of the land's produce. Relying on his judgment, and not knowing which of the products will obtain the best price, he will farm part of the land to raise flocks, produce grain, wine, hay, and so forth. The price of [63] these products will be partially dependent on the seasons and will partially depend on consumption. If wheat is plentiful relative to its consumption, it will be at a very low price; a shortage of it will lead to a high price. Is there someone who can predict the annual number of births and deaths in a state? Is there someone who can predict the growth or fall in households' expenditures? The farmer's prices for his commodities, however, naturally depend on these unpredictable events. Consequently he manages his farm's business in circumstances that are uncertain.

The city consumes more than half of the farmer's commodities. He brings them to the market there, or he sells them in the nearest town, or else some others become entrepreneurs by acting as carriers. [64] The latter have to pay a fixed price for the farmer's commodities, which is the daily market price, in order to sell them in the city at an uncertain price, which nevertheless must cover the cost of transport and leave them a profit for their business. The daily changes in the urban prices of commodities, however, though not considerable, make their profit uncertain.

The entrepreneur or merchant who transports the countryside's commodities to the city cannot stay there to retail them as they are consumed. No city family will commit itself to buying immediately all the commodities that it needs. The size of each family may vary, as may its consumption, or the family may sometimes change [65] the type of commodities that it will consume. Except for wine, families rarely stock provisions. In any case, most of the city's inhabitants live on a day-by-day basis and yet, as the largest consumers, are not in a position to stock commodities coming from the country.

For this reason several urban dwellers emerge as merchants or entrepreneurs to buy the country's produce from those who bring it, or have it brought on their account. They pay a certain price for it depending on the place where it is bought, in order to resell it, either wholesale or retail, at an uncertain price.

These entrepreneurs are wool and cereal wholesalers, bakers, butchers, manufacturers, and merchants of all [66] types who buy the country's products and materials to work and resell accordingly as the inhabitants require them for their consumption.

These entrepreneurs are never in a position to know the consumption expenditure of their city, nor for how long their customers will buy from them, given that their rivals will use all sorts of ruses to take their customers. All of this causes so much uncertainty among these entrepreneurs that it causes daily bankruptcies among them.

The manufacturer, who bought wool from the merchant or directly from the farmer, does not know the profit that he will make in his business by selling cloth and materials to the merchant draper. If the latter does not have reasonable sales, and to a lesser degree if these garments become unfashionable, he will not stock [67] the manufacturer's clothes and garments.

The draper is an entrepreneur who buys cloth and materials from the manufacturer at a certain price to sell at an uncertain price, because he cannot predict the quantity that will be consumed. It is true that he may fix a price and refuse to sell below this, but if his customers leave him so as to buy at a better price from another draper, he will face mounting bills while waiting to sell at his proposed price, and this will ruin him as soon as or sooner than if he had sold the goods without profit.

Shopkeepers and retailers of all kinds are entrepreneurs who buy at a certain price to sell in their shops, or [68] in the market, at an uncertain price. These types of entrepreneurs are encouraged and maintained in a state by consumers who, as their customers, prefer to pay a little more for the ready ability to purchase small quantities rather than having to stock goods, given that most of them do not have the means to store such stocks by purchasing them at first hand.

All of these entrepreneurs reciprocally become consumers and customers between one and another, the wine merchant with the draper and vice versa. They proportion themselves in a state to their customers or to their consumption; if there are too many hatters relative to the number of hat buyers in a city or in a street, some with the least business [69] will be made bankrupt. If there are too few, it will be an advantageous business, which will attract some new hatters to come and open up shops. In this way all types of entrepreneurs adjust themselves to risk in a state.

All the other entrepreneurs, such as those operating mines, entertainments, buildings, etc., land and sea merchants, cooks, pastrymakers, innkeepers, and also those entrepreneurs of their own labor who do not need money to establish themselves, such as journeymen craftsmen, coppersmiths, needlewomen, chimney sweeps, and water carriers, subsist in conditions of uncertainty and proportion themselves to their customers. Master craftsmen such as cobblers, tailors, carpenters, [70] wigmakers, and the like, who employ journeymen in proportion to their work, live under the same uncertainty since their customers may leave them from one day to the next. Self-employed entrepreneurs in the arts and sciences, such as painters, doctors, lawyers, and the like, practice under the same uncertainty. If an attorney or lawyer annually earns £5,000 sterling in servicing his clients or through his practice, and another only earns £500, they may both be considered to have similar uncertainty with regard to their earnings from those who employ them.

It is not part of my subject to conjecture whether all these entrepreneurs set out to make as much as they can and to dupe their customers.

By all these illustrations and [71] a multiplicity of others that can be made about this issue that concerns all the inhabitants of a state, it may be established that all the inhabitants are dependents, with the exception of the prince and the landlords; that they may be divided into two classes, namely entrepreneurs and hired people; that the entrepreneurs somehow have uncertain earnings; and that the others have fixed earnings for as long as they receive them, even though their functions and their ranks may be quite unequal. The general with his pay, the courtier with his pension, and the servant with his wage all fall into this latter category. All the others—whether they have money to establish their businesses or whether they can operate their businesses without money—are entrepreneurs and may be considered [72] as working under uncertainty. Even beggars and thieves are entrepreneurs in this category. Finally, all the state's inhabitants are dependents, deriving their subsistence and their advantages from the landlords' property.

It is true, however, that if a rich individual, or a substantial entrepreneur, has saved assets or wealth, that is, if he has stocks of wheat, wool, copper, gold or silver, or some product or merchandise for which there is a constant need or constant sales in a state, and that has a real or intrinsic value, he may then rightly be considered independent as long as this wealth lasts. He may use it to acquire a land mortgage and rents from the land and state annuities [73] when he borrows against the security of the land. He may even live much better than the owners of small estates and buy the property of some of them.

But commodities and merchandise, even gold and silver, are more subject to accidents and losses than the ownership of land. Whatever the manner by which they have been gained or saved, they have always been drawn from the current owners' land, either by gain or by the saving of earnings destined for one's subsistence.

Often, in a great state, the number of money holders may be very considerable, and although the value of all the money that circulates in the state scarcely exceeds one-ninth or one-tenth of the value of the produce drawn from the land, yet, as these money holders lend considerable sums [74] at interest, either through land mortgages or through the state's commodities and merchandise, the sums owed to them often exceed all the state's real money. They often become such an important group that, in certain cases, they could match the landlords, if the latter were not often the same money holders, and if the large money holders did not, likewise, always seek to become landlords.

It is always true, however, that the sums earned or saved are drawn from the land of the actual owners. The independence that land ownership [75] gives is limited to those who retain possession of it, as every day many of them in the state ruin themselves and others take their place, acquiring the title of their lands. Furthermore, as all the lands always have an actual master or owner, I always presume that it is from their land that the state's inhabitants derive their subsistence and all their wealth. This would not be open to question if all these owners limited themselves to living off their rents, and in such a case it would be a great deal more difficult for the other inhabitants to enrich themselves at their expense.

I will then establish it as a principle that the landlords alone are naturally independent in a state; that all the other classes are dependent on them, whether hired or entrepreneurs; and that all the state's exchange and circulation are carried out through the intervention of these entrepreneurs. [76]

14 The moods, fashions, and modes of living of the prince and, more particularly, of the landlords determine the uses to which the land is put and are responsible for variations in the market prices of all things

If the owner of a landed estate (which I wish to consider here as if it were unique in the world) farms it himself, he will pursue his desires in deciding the uses to which it will be put. (1) He will necessarily use part of it for grain in order to feed all the laborers, craftsmen, and supervisors who must work for him; and another part to raise the cattle, sheep, [77] and other animals to provide clothes, food, and other products according to the way in which he wishes to sustain them. (2) He will, according to his taste, use part of his land to create parks, gardens, orchards, or vineyards and fields for the breeding of horses that he will use for his pleasure, etc.

Now let us suppose that, to avoid all these cares and difficulties, he arranges with the supervisors of the workers to give them farms or parts of his land and leave up to them the normal care of minding the laborers that they supervise. In this way the supervisors, who thus become farmers or entrepreneurs, give the laborers, in return for their work on the land or farm, another third of the produce, as much for their food as [78] for their clothing and other products similar to those that they had when the owner directed the work. Now let us further suppose that the owner arranges with the craftsmen's supervisors the quantity of food and other products to be given to them; that he makes them become master craftsmen; that he establishes a common measure, like silver, to determine the prices at which the farmers shall sell them their wool and at which they will sell him their cloth; and that the calculations of these prices are fixed in such a way that the master craftsmen have almost the same advantages and profits that they had when they were supervisors, and that the journeymen craftsmen have also the same upkeep as before. The labor of the journeymen craftsmen will be paid either daily or by piece; the products [79] that they have made, be they hats, stockings, shoes, suits, or the like, will be reciprocally sold to the owner, the farmers, the laborers, and the other craftsmen at a price that includes all the same advantages that they enjoyed; and the farmers will sell at a price proportional to their goods and materials.

It will first emerge from this that the supervisors who have become entrepreneurs will also become the absolute masters of those who work under them, and that they will have more care and satisfaction in working in this way for their own account. After this change we suppose then that all the population of this great estate live in the same way as before. I say in consequence that all the parts and farms of this great estate will be used in the same ways [80] as they formerly were.

For if some of the farmers sowed more grain than normal in their

farms or their allotted land, it will be necessary for them to feed a lesser
number of sheep and to have less wool and mutton to sell. Consequently there will be too much grain and too little wool for the population's consumption. Then the price of wool will rise, which will
oblige people to wear their clothes for longer than normal, and there
will be a very sizable grain market and a surplus for the following year.
As it was assumed that the owner stipulated that the third of the farm's
produce owing to him be paid in money, the farmers with too much
grain and too little wool will not be in a position to pay him his rent.
If he excuses them they will take care the following year to have less
grain and more wool because the farmers need always to take care to
use their lands for those products that they believe will bring them the
highest market price. But if, [81] during the following year, they should
have too much wool and not enough grain for consumption, they will
not fail to change the use of their lands on a year-to-year basis so that
they may arrive as near as possible to proportioning their commodities
to the population's consumption. So a farmer who has just about
achieved this proportion of consumption will farm part of his land in
grass so as to have hay and another part for grain, wool, and so on, and
he will not change his approach unless he sees some considerable
change in consumption. In the current example, however, [82] we have
assumed that all the inhabitants live more or less in the same way as
they did when the owner managed his land, and that consequently the
farmers will use the land for the same purposes as they did formerly.

The owner, who has a third of the land's output available to him, is
the principal actor in the changes that may arise with respect to consumption. The laborers and craftsmen, who live on a day-to-day basis,
alter their mode of living only by necessity. If there are any well-off
farmers, master craftsmen, or other entrepreneurs who change their expenditure and consumption, they always take as their model the lords
and landlords. They imitate them with respect to clothes, food, and
[83] lifestyle. If the landlords delight in wearing fine linen, silks, or lace,
the consumption of these goods will be far greater than that of the
landlords for themselves.

If a lord or landlord who has leased out all his lands for farming decides to change his lifestyle and, for example, reduces the number of

his servants and increases his string of horses, he will cause not only his servants to leave the land in question, but also a proportionate number of craftsmen and laborers who worked for their upkeep. That part of the land used for the maintenance of these inhabitants will be used to increase his string of horses, and if all the landlords in a state did likewise, [84] they would soon increase the number of horses and reduce the population.

When an owner has dismissed a considerable number of his servants and increased his string of horses, there will be too much wheat for human consumption. Consequently the wheat will become cheap, while by contrast, hay will become dear. This will mean that the farmers will increase their grasslands and reduce the amount of wheat so as to bring it into line with its consumption. Accordingly, in this way the owners' fancies and lifestyles determine the usage of the lands and produce the changes in consumption that influence market prices. If all the landlords in a state farmed their own lands, they would use them to produce what pleased them. As the changes [85] in consumption are principally caused by their lifestyles, the market prices they offer determine all the changes that the farmers make in the lands' employment and use.

As I consider only a state in its natural and unchanging situation and do not wish to complicate my subject, I do not take into account here the changes in market prices that may arise from years of good or bad harvests, or from the extraordinary consumption produced by foreign armies or other accidents. [86]

15

The increase and decrease of the state's population depends principally on the tastes, fashions, and modes of living of the landlords

Experience shows that it is possible to multiply trees, plants, and other types of vegetables to any extent consistent with the amount of land assigned to their cultivation.

The same experience shows that it is equally possible to expand the number of every type of livestock in line with the amount of land used to feed it. If they are raised at stud, in cattle herds or flocks of sheep, [87] they will be easily increased up to that amount consistent with the quantity of land necessary to feed them. It is even possible, following the example of the Milanese, to improve the grasslands that are necessary for their upkeep through water irrigation. Hay may be harvested and used to feed a greater number of livestock by keeping them in stables rather than allowing them to feed freely off the grasslands. Sometimes, as is the case in England, sheep may be fed with turnips, so that an acre of land will feed more of them than if they only grazed on it.

In a word, it is possible to increase all sorts of livestock to the amount that it is wished to maintain, even to infinity if an unlimited amount of land is designated to feed them. The [88] multiplication of this livestock has no other limit except the means given to it for its subsistence. Undoubtedly, if all the land were used just to feed mankind, the human species would multiply to that quantity that the land could feed, in the manner that will be explained.

China ranks above every other country in terms of the expansion of its population. The poor live there uniquely on rice and rice water. They work almost naked and, in the southern provinces, they have three abundant annual rice harvests through their agricultural skills. The land never lies fallow and yields each time more than a hundredfold. Those who are clothed normally wear cotton, which requires so little [89] land for its production that an acre of land is probably sufficient to clothe five hundred adults. They all marry as their religion demands, and raise as many children as they are able to maintain. They believe it is a crime to use land for parks or ornamental gardens, considering it equivalent to defrauding people of their food. They carry travelers in sedan chairs and save working with horses through human labor. According to travelers' accounts their population is beyond belief, and yet they are forced to kill many of their children in their cradles when they realize that they have not the means to raise them, and keep only as many as they are able to feed. Through hard and determined work they catch an extraordinary amount of [90] fish in the rivers as well as farm all that is possible on the land.

Nevertheless, in years of dearth, despite the care taken by the emperor, who stockpiles rice for such occasions, they die from starvation by the thousands. Therefore, as numerous as the Chinese people are, they are necessarily proportioned to their means of subsistence, and their numbers never surpass those which the country can maintain according to their chosen lifestyle, and in accordance with this, a single acre of land suffices to maintain many of them.

On the other hand, in no other country is the increase of the population more limited than that of the savages in the interior parts of America. Living in the woods, they neglect agriculture and live from hunting the animals that they find there. There is little grass for the feeding of these animals because the forests soak up the moisture and substance of the land, and, as [91] an Indian eats many animals in a year, 50 to 100 acres of land frequently feed just one single Indian.

The hunting boundaries of a small tribe of these Indians will be limited to about forty square leagues. They wage frequent and cruel wars over these boundaries and always proportion their numbers to the means that they find for living from hunting.

The Europeans cultivate the land and draw from it the grain for their subsistence. Woolen clothing is provided from the sheep that they raise. Wheat is the grain that feeds most of them, although some peasants make their bread from rye, and in the [92] north from barley and oats. The peasants' and people's subsistence is not the same in all European countries, and the lands often vary in terms of both quality and fertility.

Without lying idle, most of the land in Flanders, and a part of that in Lombardy, yields 18 to 20 times what is sown; the Neapolitan countryside yields even more. Some French, Spanish, English, and German lands yield the same amount. Cicero teaches us that Sicilian land yielded tenfold in his time; and Pliny the Elder says that the Leontine land in Sicily yielded 100 times what was sown, Babylonian land yielded 150 times, and some African land even more.

[93] Today European land yields on average six times what is sown, so that five times the seed is available for the population's consumption. Land is normally rested in the third year, yielding wheat in the first year and barley in the second.

The supplement will show, using different assumptions about modes of living, the amount of land necessary for a person's subsistence. It will be seen there that a man who lives off bread, garlic, and roots, clothed just in hempen garments and coarse linen, wearing clogs and drinking only water, as is the case with many peasants in the southern parts of France, can subsist from the produce of one and a half acres of medium-quality land [94] yielding six times what is sown and laying fallow every three years.

On the other hand, an adult man wearing leather shoes, stockings, and woolen clothes; living in a house with a change of linen, a bed, table and chairs, and other necessary items; who drinks beer or wine moderately; and who on a daily basis eats sufficiently but reasonably meat, butter, cheese, bread, vegetables, and the like scarcely needs the product of four or five acres of land of medium quality for all of that. It is true that these calculations take into account the upkeep of only those horses necessary for plowing the earth and transporting commodities for ten miles.

History records that among the [95] first Romans, each kept their family with the produce of two journaux of land, roughly equivalent to only one Paris acre and 330 square feet. Additionally, they were almost naked, used neither wine nor oil, slept on straw, and had hardly any comfort, but they were able to draw great quantities of grain and vegetables by intensively working the land, which is quite fertile around Rome.

If the landlords wished to favor population growth by encouraging the peasants to marry young and to raise children with a promise to provide for their subsistence by limiting their lands uniquely to this purpose, they would undoubtedly increase the population up to that level that the land could support [96] according to the products of the land allotted for each person, whether it was one acre and a half or four or five acres per head.

But if, instead of this, the prince or the landlords use the land for purposes other than the upkeep of the population; if, by the market prices that they pay for commodities and merchandise, they force the farmers to use the land for purposes other than the maintenance of the population (for, as has been shown, the market prices offered by the landlords along with their consumption determine the uses to which the lands are put, similar to what would happen if they farmed the lands themselves), the population would necessarily decline. Some people, lacking employment, will be forced to leave the country; [97] others, unable to have the necessary means to raise children, will not marry or will marry later, after they have put something aside for the upkeep of the household.

If the landlords, who live in the country, move into cities far away from the lands, horses will need to be bred to transport all their food, along with that for the domestics, craftsmen, and others attracted to their city residences.

The transport of wine from Burgundy to Paris often costs more than is paid for it in the vineyards. Consequently, the land used for the upkeep of the cart horses and for their minders is greater than the land used to produce the wine and maintain those involved in producing it. [98] The greater the number of horses bred in a state, the smaller the amount of food available to its inhabitants. The upkeep of carriage horses, hunters, or chargers often costs three or four acres of land.

But when the lords and the landlords buy their cloth, silks, laces, and so forth from foreign manufacturers and pay for them by exporting their native produce to the foreigner, they reduce the population's means of subsistence very significantly and increase those of the foreigners, who often become the state's enemies.

If a Polish lord or landlord whose farmers pay him annually a rent roughly equal to one-third of his land's produce chooses himself to use Dutch cloth, linen, or the like, he will pay half his rent for this [99] merchandise and will perhaps spend the other half on other basic commodities and merchandise produced in Poland for the upkeep of his family. But in our supposition, half of his rent corresponds to one-sixth of the land's produce, and this sixth part will be carried off by the Dutch, who will be given wheat, wool, hemp, and other commodities by the Polish farmers. Here then the mode of living of the resident nobility causes one-sixth of Poland's land to be taken from its inhabitants, not to mention the feeding of cart, carriage, and charger horses that are bred in Poland, as a result of the local lord's lifestyle. Furthermore, if the farmers, with the two-thirds of the land's produce attributed to them, follow the example of their masters and consume foreign-manufactured products, [100] paid for with Poland's raw merchandise, at least one-third of the land's produce will be taken away from the population's subsistence and, what is worse, most of it will be sent to the foreigner and frequently serves to maintain the state's enemies. However initially inferior their state's manufactures may be, if the Polish landlords and lords wished to consume Polish goods only, they could, little by little, improve them, and they could maintain a greater amount of the population at work instead of giving this advantage to the foreigners; and if all states took similar care not to be the dupes of other states in trade, each state would be considerable only in proportion to its inhabitants' produce and [101] industry.

If Parisian ladies are happy to wear Brussels lace, and if France pays for this lace with champagne, it will be necessary to pay, if my calculations are right, the produce of sixteen thousand acres of vines for just one acre of flax. This will be explained more clearly elsewhere, and the calculations may be seen in the supplement. Suffice it to say here that this trade removes a great part of the land's produce from French subsistence and that all the commodities sent abroad, when the exact counterpart is not returned in exchange, tend to reduce the state's population.

When I said that the landlords could increase the population in proportion [102] to the number of people that the land could support, I assumed that most men desire nothing more than to marry, if they are enabled to maintain their families in the manner that pleases them; that is, if a man is happy with the produce of an acre and a half of land, he will marry, providing that he feels certain that he has enough to raise his family in almost the same fashion; that if the produce of only five to ten acres will satisfy him, he will not be pushed to marry, unless he believes that he will be able to keep his family in nearly the same way.

In Europe the nobility's children are reared in affluence; and, as the largest share of the property is given to the eldest son, the younger sons are in no rush to marry; [103] most of them live as bachelors, either in the army or in the monastery. But they will rarely be unwilling to marry if they are offered heiresses and fortunes, that is, the means to raise a family in the style that they envisage, and without which they would think that they would make their children unhappy.

It also arises that many men among the state's lower classes, due to pride and for reasons similar to those of the nobility, prefer to stay celibate and spend the little that they have on themselves rather than in setting up a household. But most of them would voluntarily settle if they could count on the type of assistance that they wished for their family. They would believe it injurious to their children if they raised them only to see them fall into a [104] class inferior to their own. Only a small number of people in a state avoid marriage through a spirit of libertinism; all the lower orders ask only to live, and to raise their children so that the latter may live at least as well as they do. When laborers and craftsmen do not marry, it is because they wait to save a little so as to position themselves to set up a household, or to find a girl who will bring a small sum with her to such an end, because they see every day others like them who, not taking similar precautions, set up households and fall into the most frightful poverty, being obliged to deprive themselves of their own food in order to feed their children.

It may be noted from the observations of Mr. Halley of Breslaw in Silesia that only one in six of all the females [105] of childbearing age, between sixteen and forty-five years of age, is able to actually bear a child every year, whereas Mr. Halley claims that there should be at least four out of[4] six who bear children each year, without counting those who may be sterile or who may abort. The reason that four women out of six do not bear children each year is that they cannot marry because of the discouragements and obstacles in their way. A young girl, if she

---

4. There is a problem here. The printed text of 1755 is mistaken with the words "quatre ou six." This translates as "four or six." The second edition of the *Essai* published in 1756 corrected this with the words "quatre en six." We have corrected the text to "four out of six." —AEM

is not married, takes care not to become a mother; she cannot marry if she does not find a man who wishes to run the risks of it. Most of a state's population are hired or are entrepreneurs; most are dependents; most are living under uncertainty as to whether they will find, [106] by their work or their businesses, the means to raise their households in the way they envisage. This means that not all of them marry, or, if they do, they marry so late that of the six, or at least the four, who should give birth to a child each year, effectively only one out of the six becomes a mother.

A single generation is sufficient to grow the population in line with the means of subsistence provided by the land's produce, if the landlords help to maintain households. Children do not need so much of the earth's produce as adults. Both may live, according to their consumption expenditure, from more or less of the land's produce. It has been shown that northern people, where the land is quite barren, live off so little [107] of the earth's produce that they sent colonies and swarms of men to invade the southern territories and to destroy the inhabitants so as to appropriate their lands. Depending on their mode of living, four hundred thousand people could subsist off the same produce of the land that normally maintains only a hundred thousand. Indeed, a man who consumes the produce of only one and a half acres of land will perhaps be more robust and braver than the person who consumes the produce of five to ten acres. Therefore it appears to me that enough inductions have been made to understand that a state's population depends on the means of subsistence, and since the means of subsistence depend on the care and uses made of the land, and that these uses are principally reliant [108] on the pleasures, tastes, and mode of living of the landlords, so it is clear that the growth or decrease in the population depends on the landlords.

The increase in the population may be greatest in the countries where people are content to live very poorly and to use the least of the land's produce. But it would not be possible to support so many people in countries where the peasants and laborers often eat meat, drink wine or beer, and so forth.

Sir William Petty, and after him Mr. Davenant, Inspector of the English Customs, appear to stray from nature when they attempt to measure the growth of population by progressive generations since Adam, the first father. Their calculations appear to be purely [109] imaginary and randomly compiled. How can they satisfactorily explain the decline of these huge populations that were formerly in Asia, Egypt, and even Europe, on the basis of their observations of the actual birth rates in certain districts? If it is observed that seventeen centuries ago there were twenty-six million people in Italy, now reduced to at most six million, how can one determine from the progressions of Mr. King that England, with a current population of five to six million people, will probably have thirteen million in a certain number of years? We see that the English in general consume each day more of the land's produce than their forefathers, which in truth is why there are [110] fewer inhabitants than in the past.

Men multiply like mice in a barn if they have unlimited means of subsistence. The English in the Colonies will become proportionately more numerous in three generations than their counterparts in England in thirty because they find new lands in the Colonies to cultivate once they have chased the savages from them.

All countries at all times have witnessed wars for land and for the means of subsistence. The savages and civilized nations quickly rebuild the population when peace has been restored after wars have destroyed or reduced the population of a country, especially when the prince and landlords give it their encouragement.

A state that has conquered several [111] provinces may acquire an increase in the subsistence of its people through the levy that it imposes on its conquered people. The Romans drew a great part of their subsistence from Egypt, Sicily, and Africa, and this is what caused Italy to have so many people.

A state that has mines and exports manufactures requiring little of the land's produce to foreign countries, and which, in return, imports considerable merchandise and products of the land, acquires an increased fund for the subsistence of its subjects.

The Dutch generally exchange with foreigners their labor, from either shipping or fisheries or manufactures, for the products [112] of the land. Without this, Holland would be unable to maintain independently half of its population. England purchases considerable quantities of wood, hemp, and other materials or products from the soil from foreign countries, and consumes a great amount of wine, which it pays for with minerals, manufactures, etc. This enables it to save on a great amount of the land's produce. Without these advantages, knowing the expenditure needed for the upkeep of its people, the population could not be as numerous as it is. The coal mines save them many millions of acres that otherwise would be required to produce timber.

But all of these advantages are refinements and exceptions, which I mention only in passing. The natural [113] and usual way to increase the number of people in a state is to give them employment and to use the lands to provide for their maintenance.

The question as to whether it is better to have a great number of poor and inadequately maintained people rather than a smaller number living at their ease—a million people consuming the produce of six acres per head, or four million who live off the produce of an acre and a half—is also outside of my subject.

16

*The more labor in a state,
the greater the extent that it is
considered naturally wealthy*

It is easy to see from a long calculation in the supplement [114] that the work of twenty-five adult people is sufficient to provide a hundred other adults with all the necessities for living according to our European standard of consumption. It is true that these calculations for food, clothing, and lodgings are rough and elementary, but there is ease and abundance here. It may be assumed that a third of the people in a state are too young or too old for daily work and furthermore that one-sixth of them are made up of landlords, sick people, and different types of entrepreneurs, who do not provide the manual labor for the different needs of the people. All of these together constitute one-half of the population who are without work, or without the work they should be doing: thus, if twenty-five people [115] provide the work necessary for the other hundred, there remain twenty-five people out of that hundred who are available to work and who will have nothing to do.

Soldiers and servants in wealthy families will be among these twenty-five people, and if the others are employed in additional work to refine those things necessary for living, such as the production of fine linen and sheets, the state will be deemed to be rich in proportion to the increase in this work, even though it adds nothing to the quantity of things necessary for people's subsistence and upkeep.

Work increases the taste for food and drink. Finely wrought knives and forks are valued more than those [116] that are roughly and hastily produced. The same may be said about a house, a bed, a table, and generally everything that is necessary for a comfortable living.

It is a matter of indifference in a state whether people are used to wearing coarse or fine clothes, provided that both last for a similar length of time, and whether they eat in a sophisticated or crude manner, as long as they live well and have enough, given that drink, food, and clothing are equally consumed whether they are finely or roughly prepared, and that nothing remains in the state of these types of wealth.

But it is always true that the states where fine clothes and linen are worn, and where people eat properly and with refinement, are richer [117] and better considered than those where all of these things are ruder, and furthermore that the more populous states living in the style of the former are better considered than those where one sees proportionately less.

But if the 25 percent of the people that we have discussed were employed in producing durable goods such as those drawn from the iron, lead, pewter, and copper mines, etc., and if they were working them to produce tools and instruments for the use of people, such as vases, plates, and other useful things that last longer than earthenware, the state would not only appear to be richer, but will be so in reality.

It will definitely be so if these people are employed to mine gold and silver from the earth. These metals [118] are not only durable, but are, so to speak, permanent in that they cannot be destroyed by fire and are usually considered exchangeable for all that is necessary in life. Their work will be equally useful and will genuinely improve the state if these people attract gold and silver into it in exchange for manufactures and products that they export abroad.

The point indeed that appears to determine the comparative greatness of states is the reserve stock that they have over and above their annual consumption, comprising stores of clothes, linen, corn, and so forth to serve when necessary in years of dearth or war. This is the case to a greater extent when the real reserve stock is gold and silver—the greater or smaller actual quantity of which necessarily determines the comparative greatness of kingdoms and states—as gold and silver may always [119] be used to buy these things, even from the state's enemies.

If a country normally brings in gold and silver from abroad through the export of the state's merchandise and of products such as wheat, wine, wool, etc., this will not fail to enrich the state at the cost of a reduction in its population. But that state will be usefully and significantly enriched if gold and silver are brought in from abroad in exchange for its population's work on manufactures and products that contain little taken from the earth. It is true that in a great state it would not be feasible to employ the 25 percent of the population, discussed above, [120] to produce goods that can be consumed abroad. For example, a million men will make more cloth than will be consumed annually in the commercial world, because the majority of people in each country are always clothed from the country's raw material. Rarely will a state be found where a hundred thousand people are employed to clothe foreigners. This is shown in the supplement, with reference to England, which is the leading country in Europe with respect to the amount of cloth that is furnished to foreigners.

A strong and valuable domestic consumption of the state's manufactures is necessary to ensure a sizable foreign consumption for them. It is necessary to discourage [121] all foreign manufactures and to provide plenty of employment for the people.

If it is not possible to find enough employment to occupy them on useful and advantageous things for the state, I have no objection to encouraging this 25 percent of the population to provide work that serves solely for ornament or amusement. The state is considered no less rich by the thousands of toys that trick the attention of ladies and even men, and that provide the games and attractions that we see, than by useful and serviceable products. It is said that, during the siege of Corinth, when everybody was busy, Diogenes started to roll his barrel to make it appear that he was not lazy. Today we have whole groups of people, both men and women, who are working [122] and exercising on jobs just as useless to the state as that of Diogenes. As long as it is not possible to employ a man usefully, it is worthwhile to encourage him to work, no matter how little he brings to the ornament or even the amusement of a state.

It is always the landlords' inspiration that encourages or discourages the different occupations of people and the different types of work that they invent.

The example of the prince, who is copied by his court, normally determines the inspiration and tastes of the other landlords in general. The example of the latter naturally influences all the lower orders. Thus, it is obvious that the prince, by his sole example and without any constraint, can give [123] whatever turn he wishes to his subjects' labor.

There would be almost no cities if each landlord in a state possessed just a small amount of land similar to that which would normally be worked by a single farmer. The people would be more numerous, and the state would be very rich, if each of the owners engaged for some useful work the people fed by his land.

But when the nobles have great amounts of land, they necessarily encourage luxury and laziness. Providing a state could exist in a continuous peace, it would be a matter of indifference to it whether an abbot, at the head of a congregation of fifty monks, lived off the produce of many fine estates, [124] or a nobleman, with fifty servants and horses used just for his service, lived off these lands.

But a nobleman along with his retinue and horses is useful to a state in times of war. He can always be useful to the magistrature, and he can help maintain order in the state during peacetime. He is a great presence in all situations, whereas, as one says, the monks are not of any utility or are not seen in peace or war on this side of paradise.

Mendicant friars' monasteries are far more dangerous to a state than those of the closed orders. The latter normally do no harm, other than occupying the lands that could be used to provide the state with officers and magistrates, unlike the mendicant friars who have no useful work and often interrupt and prevent other people from working. They [125] extract alms from the poor, which subsistence the latter need to be fit for their work. They make them lose a great deal of time in useless conversations, without mentioning those who ingratiate themselves into families, and those who are corrupt. Experience shows that the states that embraced Protestantism, and which have neither monks nor mendicants, have visibly become more powerful. They benefit also from having suppressed a great number of feasts that prevent people in Catholic countries from working, and that reduce by an eighth the annual amount of labor the people carry out.

It appears to me that, if one wished to use all the resources in a state, it should be possible to reduce the number of mendicants by transferring them to monasteries, according to the vacancies [126] or deaths that occurred there, without excluding from these retreats those who could not show examples of their skill in the speculative sciences but who are capable of advancing the practical arts, that is, some parts of mathematics. According to what was established in the preceding chapter, the celibacy of church people is not as disadvantageous as is commonly believed; but their idleness is most damaging.

17 Of metals and money, particularly gold and silver

Just as the land yields more or less wheat according to its fertility and the labor applied to it, so also the iron, lead, tin, gold, and silver [127] mines, and the like produce more or less of these metals according to the richness of these mines and the quantity and quality of the labor working them, either in digging, or draining, or smelting and refining, and so forth. The high rate of mortality in the silver mines makes the labor expensive, given that people can rarely spend more than five or six years in this labor.

Like all things, the real or intrinsic value of metals is proportional to the land and labor necessary for their production. The expense of the land for this production is great only to the extent that the mine owner can obtain a profit from the miners' work when the veins are found to be unusually rich. The land necessary for the upkeep of the miners and the workers, that is, [128] the labor of the mine, constitutes the principal expense and, often, the ruin of the entrepreneur.

As is the case for all merchandise and commodities, the market value of metals is sometimes above and sometimes below their intrinsic value, and varies in line with their abundance or scarcity, according to the consumption of them.

If the landlords, and the other lower orders in a state that imitate them, should reject the use of tin and copper, because of the mistaken belief that they are dangerous to health, and if they all used earthenware dishes and utensils, these metals would be at a very low market price, and the labor used to extract them from the mine would cease. [129] But as these metals are found to be useful, and serve for all types of human activities, they will always have a market value that will correspond to their abundance or rarity, and the expenditure on them. They will always be mined to replace what is lost in daily use.

Iron is not only practical for the daily uses of communal life, but one could say that it is in a certain sense necessary. It is sure that if the Americans, who did not use it before the discovery of their continent, had discovered iron in the mines, and known its uses, that they would have worked to produce this metal no matter the expense that it would have cost them.

Gold and silver are capable of providing not only the same uses as tin and copper, but [130] even most of those served by lead and iron. They have this further advantage with respect to other metals in that they cannot be destroyed by fire, and they are so durable that they may be regarded as permanent materials. It is therefore not surprising that men, who found the other metals useful, should have prized gold and silver even before they were used in exchange. From the foundation of Rome the Romans valued them, though they did not use them as money until five hundred years later. Perhaps all the other nations did likewise, and did not adopt these metals as money until a long time after they had been used for other purposes. The most ancient historians, however, indicate that gold and [131] silver served as money in Egypt and Asia from time immemorial, and we learn from the Book of Genesis that silver monies were made from the time of Abraham.

Let us now assume that silver was first discovered in a mine on Mount Niphates in Mesopotamia. It is natural to believe that one or more of the landlords, finding this metal to be beautiful and useful, first made use of it and willingly encouraged the miner or the entrepreneur to extract more from the mine, giving him in exchange for his work and that of his assistants as much of the earth's produce as was needed for their maintenance. As in Mesopotamia this metal became more and more valued, while the large owners bought silver ewers, the lower orders could buy silver cups, [132] according to their means and savings. Undoubtedly the mine's entrepreneur, perceiving a continuous sale of his merchandise, apportioned to it a value equivalent to its weight and quality against the other goods or merchandise that he received in exchange for it. While everyone looked at this metal as a precious and durable thing, and attempted to possess some pieces of it, the entrepreneur, who alone distributed it, was in a way the master in demanding in exchange an arbitrary quantity of other goods and merchandise for it.

Now let us suppose that, beyond the river Tigris, and consequently outside Mesopotamia, a new mine was discovered with veins vastly richer and more abundant than those of Mount Niphates, [133] and that the work on this easily drained mine was less demanding than the first.

It is natural to believe that this new mine's entrepreneur was able to provide silver at a far lower price than that of Mount Niphates, and that the Mesopotamian people, desiring to have silver pieces and objects, might find it in their interest to export their merchandise outside the country and to give it to the new mine's entrepreneur in exchange for this metal, rather than to exchange it with the original entrepreneur. The latter, facing falling sales, would necessarily lower his price, but the new entrepreneur, proportionately reducing his own, would force the original entrepreneur out of work, and then the silver prices for all other goods and merchandise would necessarily [134] be determined by those fixed at the new mine. Silver would then cost less to the people beyond the Tigris than to those of Mesopotamia, because the latter were obliged to pay the costs of the long-distance transport involved in acquiring silver for their goods and merchandise.

It is easy to see that, when several silver mines were discovered and the landlords had acquired a taste for this metal, they were imitated by the other orders, and that bits and pieces of silver, even when un-worked, were eagerly sought after because nothing was easier than to make what one wanted of them, according [135] to their weight and quantity. As this metal was valued at least according to its cost of pro-duction, several people who possessed it, finding themselves in some difficulties, might pawn it so as to borrow the things that they required, and even sell it outright later; the practice of fixing its value in propor-tion to its quantity, that is, its weight relative to all types of goods and merchandise, emerged from this. But as silver may be alloyed with iron, lead, tin, copper, and other metals that are less rare and that may be mined at lower cost, the silver trade was subject to a great deal of fraud, and this resulted in many kingdoms establishing mints to certify by a public coinage the true quantity [136] of silver in each coin, and to give to individuals, who brought silver bars or ingots to it, the same quantity of coin bearing a stamp or certificate of the true amount of silver contained therein.

The cost of these certificates or mintings is sometimes paid for by the public or by the prince. It is the method that was followed in an-cient Rome and is followed today in England; sometimes, as is the practice in France, those who bring the silver to be minted bear the costs of minting it.

Pure silver is rarely found in the mines. In ancient times they did not know how to refine it in the purest manner. They always minted fine silver coins, and yet those still extant from the Greeks, Romans, [137] Jews, Asiatics, and others are never found to be perfectly pure. Today there is more skill, and the secret of refining pure silver is known. The different methods of refining it are not part of my subject. Many au-thors have dealt with it, among whom is Mr. Boizard. I will confine myself to observing that there are many costs associated with refining, and that is the reason for preferring one ounce of pure silver to two ounces of silver that contain one-half of copper or another alloy. It is expensive to separate this alloy and to produce one ounce of silver from these two ounces, whereas by a simple melting it is possible to alloy all other metals with silver in whatever proportion desired. If, sometimes, pure silver is alloyed with copper, it is just to make it more malleable [138] and suitable for the objects made of it. But in the valuation of all silver, the copper or alloy counts for nothing, and only the quantity of fine and pure silver is considered. On account of this an assay is always taken to determine the amount of pure silver.

Assaying is nothing other than refining a small piece of a silver bar, for example, that one wishes to assay, so as to learn how much pure silver it contains, and to judge the complete bar by this small piece. A small piece is thus cut from the bar, of twelve grains, for example, and is precisely weighed on balances that are so accurate that it sometimes takes only one one-thousandth part of a grain to make them imbalance. Then it is refined by aqua fortis, or by heat; that is, the copper [139] or the alloy is removed from it. When the silver is pure it is re-weighed on the same balance, and if the weight is then found to be eleven grains rather than the former twelve, the assayer says that the bar is eleven parts of pure silver, that is, it contains eleven parts of pure silver and one part of copper or alloy. This will again be understood more easily by those who are interested in examining these assays. There is nothing else mysterious about it. Gold is assayed in the same way, with the only difference being that the degrees of fineness of gold are divided into twenty-four parts called carats, because gold is more precious. These carats are divided into thirty-two parts, while the degrees of fineness of silver are divided into only twelve parts called deniers, and these deniers have twenty-four grains each.

[140] Custom has conferred on gold and on silver the term intrinsic value, so as to designate and indicate the quantity of pure gold or silver contained in a bar. In this essay, however, due to my inability to find another term more suitable to express my thought, I have always used the term intrinsic value to establish the quantity of land and labor involved in production. Let it be understood that I give this warning only

so as to avoid any misunderstanding. When not discussing gold and silver, the term will always apply without any equivocation.

We have seen that metals such as gold, silver, and iron have many uses and that they have a real value proportional to the land and labor involved in their production. We shall see, in the [141] second part of this essay, that men were forced by necessity to use a common measure to determine the proportion and the value of commodities and merchandise that they wished to exchange. The only question to consider is which commodity or merchandise should be the most appropriate for this common measure, and whether it was not necessity, rather than taste, that created this preference for gold, silver, and copper, which are generally used for this purpose today.

Ordinary commodities such as corn, wine, and meat do have a real value and serve the needs of life, but they are all perishable and even inconvenient to transport, and consequently, they are unsuitable to act as a common measure.

[142] Goods such as cloth, linen, and leather are also perishable and may not be subdivided without changing in some way their value in use for people. Like raw materials they involve considerable transport costs and are even expensive to store. Consequently, they are not really appropriate to serve as a common measure.

Diamonds and other precious stones, even assuming they had no intrinsic value and were assessed only by taste, would be suitable to serve as a common measure but for the fact that they can be counterfeited and cannot be divided without loss. But these defects, along with their inappropriateness for common use, mean that they cannot serve as a common measure.

[143] Iron, which is quite durable and always useful, could serve well in the absence of others that are better. It can be destroyed by fire, and is quantitatively too bulky. It was used from the time of Lycurgus up to the Peloponnesian War, but as its value was necessarily determined intrinsically, or in proportion to the land and labor required for its production, a great quantity of it was needed for a small value. It was strange that, in order to limit its use just for exchange, its quality was spoiled through the use of vinegar, thereby making it redundant for ordinary use and reserving it for exchange. Thus it was of use only to

the austere Spartans, and was even discontinued by them once they developed links with other countries. To destroy the [144] Spartans all that was needed was to discover rich iron mines and make money like theirs in order to buy their commodities and merchandise, while they could obtain nothing from abroad in return for their spoiled iron. As a result, concerned only with war, they developed no foreign trade.

Lead and tin have a disadvantage similar to that of iron in that they are bulky and can be destroyed by fire, but in a case of necessity, they could be used for exchange if copper was not more suitable and more durable.

Copper alone served as money for the Romans until the year 484 after the foundation of Rome. It is still used in Sweden today, even for substantial payments. It is, however, too bulky for very large [145] payments, and the Swedes themselves prefer to be paid in gold and silver rather than in copper.

In the American Colonies tobacco, sugar, and cocoa have served as money, but these commodities are too bulky and perishable and of unequal quality. Consequently, they are not very useful in serving as money or as a common measure of value.

Gold and silver alone are small in volume, equal in quality, easy to transport, divisible without loss, easy to keep, beautiful and brilliant in the articles made of them, and durable almost until eternity. All those who have used other things for money revert to them as soon as they can acquire enough of them for their exchanges. Gold and silver [146] are inconvenient for only the smallest transactions. Gold and even silver coins worth a liard or a denier would be too small to be easily handled. It is said that the Chinese, involved in small transactions, used scissors to cut off thin slices of the silver that they weighed. But since they started trading with Europe they have started to use copper for these occasions.

It is not surprising, then, that all nations came to use gold and silver as money or as the common measure of value, along with copper for small change. Their decision was determined by utility and necessity rather than by taste or consent. The production of silver necessitates a considerable and expensive amount of labor. [147] The expensiveness of silver miners is caused by a very high mortality, as they rarely survive five or six years of this labor. Hence a small silver coin corresponds to as much land and labor as a large copper coin.

Money, or the common measure of value, must correspond, really and intrinsically, in land and labor prices, to the articles exchanged for it. Otherwise it would have only an imaginary value. For example, if a prince or a republic authorized as legal tender something that had no real and intrinsic value, not only would the other states refuse to accept it on this basis, but the population itself would reject it on perceiving [148] its lack of real value. When, toward the end of the first Punic War, the Romans wished to give to the copper *as* of two ounces' weight the same value as that previously given to the *as* of one pound's or twelve ounces' weight, it could not be maintained for long in exchange. History universally shows that when princes have debased their money while keeping it at the same nominal value, all merchandise and raw material prices increased proportionately with the debasement of monies.

Mr. Locke says that public consent has given its value to gold and silver. This is not to be doubted, since absolute necessity played no part in it. It is the same consent that has given, [149] and continues every day to give, a value to lace, linen, fine cloths, copper, and other metals. In absolute terms people could subsist without any of these things. But it should not be concluded from this that all things have only an imaginary value. They have a value proportional to the land and labor that enter into their production. Gold and silver, like other merchandise and commodities, can be produced only at costs proportional to the value roughly given to them. In addition, whatever men produce by their labor, it is necessary that this labor provide for their upkeep. This is the great principle that one hears every day from the mouths of the lower classes, who are not involved in [150] our observations, and who live by their work or by their enterprises. *Everybody must live.*

End of the first part.

Part 2

I *Of barter*

In the preceding part, an attempt was made to prove that the real value of all things used by mankind is proportional to the quantity of [152] land used for their production and for the upkeep of those who produced it. In this second part, I will begin by summing up the different degrees of fertility of the land in a number of countries, and the different types of commodities that it can produce with greater abundance according to its intrinsic quality. Then, after assuming the establishment of towns and their markets to facilitate the sale of those commodities, the impossibility of fixing their respective intrinsic values will be shown by comparing the exchanges that can be made for wine against cloth, for wheat against shoes, hats, and so forth, and by the difficulty involved in transporting these different commodities or merchandise. Mankind [153] found itself obliged to find something that was easily transportable, not perishable, and having by weight a proportion, or a value, equal to the different commodities and merchandise, whether necessary or convenient. The choice of gold and silver emerged from this for large transactions, and that of copper for smaller ones.

These metals are not only durable and easily transportable, but correspond to the employment of a considerable area of land for their production, which gives them the true value that people seek in an equivalent.

Mr. Locke, who, like all the other English writers who have written on this subject, is concerned only with market prices, establishes that the value of all things is proportional to their abundance or their scarcity and to the abundance or scarcity [154] of the silver for which they are exchanged. It is generally known that prices of commodities and merchandise have increased in Europe since the imports of a great quantity of silver from the West Indies.

In my opinion, though, it should not be generally believed that the market price of things should be proportional to their quantity and to the actual amount of silver that circulates in one place, because the commodities and merchandise that are sent off to be sold elsewhere do not influence the prices of those that remain. If, for example, in a town possessing double the amount of wheat that is consumed, a comparison is made of this entire quantity of wheat with the amount of silver, then the wheat would be proportionally more abundant than the money destined to purchase it. Yet, the market price [155] will be maintained just as if there was only half this amount of wheat, because the other half can be, and even has to be, sent to the city. The costs of transportation will be included in the city's price, which is always proportionally higher than that of the town. But, aside from the case of hoping to sell in another market, I find that Mr. Locke's idea is right only in the sense [explained in] the following chapter, and not otherwise.

2   *Of market prices*

Let us assume that there are butchers on one side and buyers on the other. The price of meat will be determined after some bargaining. A pound of beef will be approximately valued in silver [156] in the same way that all the meat presented for sale in the market is to all the silver brought there to purchase beef.

This proportion is determined by bargaining. The butcher sets his price by the number of buyers that he sees; the buyers, on their side, offer less if they feel that the butcher will have smaller sales: the price fixed by some is usually followed by others. Some butchers are better at marketing their merchandise; other buyers are more adept at running it down. Although this method of fixing market prices has no exact or geometrical basis, because it often depends on the eagerness or readiness of a small number of buyers and sellers, it does not appear that it could be arrived at in any more [157] convenient way. It is clear that the quantity of commodities or merchandise suitable for sale, proportioned to the demand or the quantity of buyers, is the basis on which is fixed, or always assumed to be fixed, the actual market prices, and that generally speaking these prices do not vary much from the intrinsic value.

Let us make further suppositions. At the start of the season, several stewards have been given orders to buy green peas. One steward has ordered the purchase of 10 quarts for 60 livres, another 10 quarts for 50 livres, a third 10 for 40 livres, and a fourth 10 for 30 livres. It would be necessary to have a market of 40 quarts of green peas for all of these orders to be executed. Let us assume that there are only 20: the sellers, seeing many buyers, [158] will keep up their prices, and the buyers will offer those consistent with their orders, so that those offering 60 livres for 10 quarts will be the first to be served. The sellers, then seeing that no one wishes to offer more than 50 livres, will release the other 10 quarts at this price, but those given orders not to exceed 30 or 40 livres will return empty-handed.

If, instead of 40 quarts, there are 400, not only will the stewards be able to buy the green peas below their order prices, but the sellers, wishing to be preferred by the small number of buyers, will lower their green peas to almost their intrinsic value, and in this case many stewards who had no orders will buy them.

[159] It frequently occurs that sellers, because of their eagerness to keep up their market prices, miss the opportunity to sell their commodities or merchandise advantageously and lose by this. It also happens that by maintaining their prices they will often be able to sell more advantageously another day.

Distant markets may always influence domestic market prices: if wheat is extremely expensive in France, it will rise in England and other neighboring countries.

3   *Of the circulation of money*

It is generally believed in England that a farmer must make three rents. The first is the principal and true rent that he pays [160] to the owner, which is supposed to be equal to one-third of the produce of his farm; the second is a rent for his upkeep and that of the men and horses that he uses to cultivate the farm; and, finally, the third is a rent that should go to him so as to make his business profitable.

The same idea generally prevails in the other European countries, although in some, such as that of Milan, the farmer gives half of the land's produce, instead of a third, to the owner. Furthermore, many landlords in all countries attempt to push up the rents as high as possible, but the farmers are normally very poor when they are charged more than one-third of the produce. I am persuaded that the Chinese owner takes more than three-quarters of the land's produce from his farmer.

[161] When a farmer has some funds to manage his farm's business, however, the owner, who rents his farm for one-third of the produce, will be sure of his payment and will be better positioned from such an agreement than if he rented his farm at a higher price to a poor farmer, thereby running the risk of not receiving his rent. The larger the farm, the more prosperous the farmer will be. This is to be seen in England, where the farmers are normally more prosperous than in other countries where the farms are smaller.

The assumption that I will follow in my analysis of the circulation of money is that the farmers make three rents and spend the third rent on living more comfortably rather than saving it. This in effect is the situation of [162] most farmers in all countries.

All the products of a state come, directly or indirectly, from the farmers; so do all of the materials from which the products are made. With the exception of fish, it is the land that produces all things, and even then the fishermen who catch the fish must be maintained with the produce of the land.

The farmer's three rents must then be considered as the principal sources, or, it might be said, the first mover behind circulation in the state. The first rent must be paid to the owner in ready money; ready money is necessary, for the second and third rents, to buy iron, tin, copper, salt, sugar, cloth, and generally all of the city's merchandise that is consumed [163] in the country; but all of that hardly exceeds a sixth part of the total of the three rents. Cash is generally unnecessary to pay for the food and drink of people living in the countryside.

The farmer can brew his own beer or make his own wine without spending ready money. He can make his bread, kill his cattle, sheep, pigs, and so forth, which are eaten in the countryside. He can pay most of his assistants in wheat, meat, and drink, not only the laborers but also the country craftsmen, by evaluating his produce from the nearest market prices and their labor by its usual local price.

Food, clothing, and lodgings are the necessities of life. As has been explained, it is not necessary [164] to have cash to obtain food in the countryside. If, as is often the case, coarse linen and cloths are made there, and houses are built there, the labor for all of this may be paid through negotiated barter without the need to use any money.

The only money required in the countryside will be that needed to pay for the principal rent to the owner, and for the merchandise that country people necessarily acquire from the city, such as knives, scissors, pins, needles, cloth for some farmers or other well-off people, kitchen utensils, plates, and generally all that is brought from the city.

I have already observed the estimate that half of the inhabitants of a state live in the [165] cities, and that consequently they purchase more than half the land's produce. Cash is therefore needed not only for the owner's rent, which corresponds to a third of the produce, but also for the city's merchandise consumed by the countryside, which corresponds to something more than a sixth of the land's produce. But then one-third and one-sixth represent one-half of the produce; consequently the ready money that circulates in the countryside must be equal to at least half of the land's produce, which means that the other half, or somewhat less, may be consumed in the countryside without the need for cash.

The circulation of this money occurs when the owners purchase retail goods in the [166] city with the bulk rental payments made by the farmers, and the city's entrepreneurs, such as the butchers, the bakers, and the brewers, little by little acquire this same money to purchase cattle, wheat, barley, and the like in bulk from the farmers. In consequence large monetary payments are distributed in small amounts, and all the small amounts are then amassed to make bulk sum payments, either directly or indirectly, to the farmers. This money always passes in payment, as much at the retail as at the wholesale level.

When I remarked that it was necessary to have an amount of money for the countryside's circulation often equal to half of the land's produce, this is the minimum; and to ensure that the countryside's circulation is carried out with ease, I [167] will assume that the cash necessary to carry out the circulation of the three rents is equal in value to two of these rents, or equal to two-thirds of the land's produce. It will be later seen, through various illustrations, that this assumption is not too far from the truth.

Let us now assume that the money that drives the circulation of a small state is equal to 10,000 silver ounces, and that all payments in this money, from the countryside to the city and from the city to the countryside, are made once a year; and that these 10,000 silver ounces are equal in value to two-thirds of the farmer's rents or two-thirds of the land's produce. The rents of the owners will correspond to 5,000 ounces, and all the monetary circulation remaining between those in the countryside and those in the city, [168] requiring annual payments, will also correspond to 5,000 ounces.

But if the owners contract with their farmers for half-yearly rather than annual payments, and if the debtors of the two other rents pay them every six months too, this change in payment practices will alter the pace of circulation; and whereas 10,000 ounces were formerly required for once-a-year payments, now only 5,000 are needed, because 5,000 ounces paid twice will have the same effect as 10,000 ounces paid once.

Furthermore, if the owners contract with their farmers for quarterly payments, or if they are happy to receive rents from their farmers according as the four seasons of the year [169] enable them to sell their commodities, and if all other payments are made quarterly, only 2,500 ounces will be required for the same circulation that would have necessitated 10,000 ounces for annual payments. Consequently, if it is assumed that all payments are made on a quarterly basis in the small state in question, the proportion of the value of money necessary for circulation is to the annual produce of the soil—that is, to the three rents—as 2,500 livres is to 15,000 livres, or as 1 to 6, so that money would correspond to one-sixth of the land's annual produce.

But given that entrepreneurs carry out each branch of circulation in the cities; that the consumption of food is made by daily, weekly, or [170] monthly payments; that the payment for the clothing of families, purchased biannually or annually, is made at different times by different people; that for most people the payment for drink is made on a daily basis; and that payment for small beer, coal, and thousands of other types of consumption is immediately made, it would appear that the proportion that has been established for quarterly payments may be too high, and that it would be possible to carry out the circulation of the land's produce of 15,000 ounces of silver with much less than 2,500 ounces of silver coins.

As the farmers need to make large payments at least every quarter to the owners, however, and as the taxes that the [171] prince or the state receives from consumption are accumulated by the collectors in order to pay the receivers-general, it is necessary to have a sufficient quantity of cash in circulation so that these large payments can be easily made, without hindering the circulation of currency relating to the food and clothing of the people.

It will be understood from what I have been saying that the proportion of cash necessary for circulation in a state is not an incomprehensible thing, and that this quantity may be greater or smaller in states depending on the lifestyle that is followed and the rapidity of payments. But it is very difficult to be specific with respect to the quantity in general, as the proportion may differ in different countries. [172] It is only conjectural when I say that generally, "The ready money necessary to carry out the circulation and exchange in a state is almost equal in value to one-third of the annual rents of the landlords."

This proportion will not vary much in a state whether money is scarce or abundant, because in the states where money is abundant the land is rented at a higher price and at a lower one in those where money is scarcer. This is a rule that will always be found to be true. But it is normally the case that there is more barter in states where money is scarcer than in those where money is more abundant, and that consequently circulation is faster and less delayed in states where money is not so [173] scarce. As a result the rapidity of circulation must always be considered in calculating the amount of money in circulation.

Assuming that the money in circulation is equal to one-third of all the landlords' rents and that these rents are equal to one-third of the annual produce of these same lands, it follows that "the money that circulates in a state is equal in value to one-ninth of all the land's produce."

Sir William Petty, in a manuscript of 1685, often assumes, without giving any reasons, that the money in circulation is equal in value to one-tenth of the land's produce. I believe that this is an opinion that he developed through the experience and practical knowledge that he had, of both the money then circulating in Ireland, where he had surveyed most [174] of the lands, and the commodities that he was able to estimate by mere observation. I am not too far from his view, but I chose to compare the quantity of money in circulation to the owners' rents, which are normally paid in money, and the value of which may be more easily known by an equal land tax, rather than to compare the amount of money to commodities or the land's products, whose prices vary daily in the markets, and of which a considerable quantity are consumed without ever passing through these markets. To strengthen my case I will give several reasons, backed up by examples, in the next chapter. Though this will not be found to be exactly the case in each state, nevertheless I believe it to be useful. It suffices if it approximates the truth and if it prevents the [175] states' leaders from forming extravagant ideas about the quantity of money in circulation. There is no area of knowledge more prone to delusion than that of statistics when they are dependent on the use of the imagination, just as there is no area of knowledge more convincing when they are based on detailed facts.

There are cities and countries that possess no land and that subsist by exchanging their labor and manufactures for the land products of others: such are Hamburg, Danzig, some other imperial cities, and even a part of Holland. It appears more difficult to estimate circulation in these states. But if it were possible to quantify the amount of foreign land necessary for their subsistence, the calculation would probably not differ [176] from that which I made for the other states that live principally from their own products and that are the subject of this essay.

As to the amount of cash necessary to carry out foreign trade, it appears that no more is required than the amount that circulates in the state when its balance of trade with other countries is equal, that is, when the commodities and merchandise that are exported are equal in value to those that are imported.

If France exports cloth to Holland and in return imports spices for the same value, the owner who purchases these spices pays the value to the grocer, and the grocer pays this same value to the cloth manufacturer, who is owed this same value in Holland for the cloth that he sends there. [177] This is transacted through bills of exchange, the nature of which I will explain later. In France the landlord's rent is not linked to these two monetary payments, and no money leaves France on that account. All the other classes that consume Dutch spices pay the grocer in the same way; namely, those who live from the first rent— that is, originating from the landlord—pay for them with the money from the first rent, and those who live from the other two rents, either in the countryside or in the city, pay the grocer, either directly or indirectly, with money originating from the circulation of these two rents. The grocer then pays this money to the manufacturer for his bills of exchange drawn on Holland. When the balance of this trade is equal, there is no need for an increase in money for circulation [178] in the state due to foreign trade. But if this balance of trade is not equal— in other words, if more merchandise is exported to Holland than is imported, or if more is imported than exported—money is required for the surplus that Holland must send to France or that France sends to Holland. This will either increase or reduce the amount of money circulating in France.

It may even happen that, when the balance is equal with a foreign country, this trade may retard the circulation of cash and consequently necessitate a greater quantity of money because of this trade.

For example, if French ladies wearing French fabrics wish to wear Dutch velvets that are [179] paid for by the cloth sent to Holland, they will buy these velvets from merchants who have imported them from Holland, and these merchants will pay the cloth manufacturers. This means that the money passes through more hands than if the ladies paid the manufacturers with their money and contented themselves with French fabrics. When the same money passes through the hands of many entrepreneurs, the rapidity of circulation is slowed down. But it is difficult to make an exact estimate of these types of delay, which are dependent on various circumstances. Thus, in the current example, if the ladies pay the merchant for the velvet today, and if tomorrow the merchant pays the manufacturer for his bill of exchange drawn on Holland, and if the next day the manufacturer pays the wool merchant and the next day the latter pays the farmer, [180] it could happen that the farmer will hold the money for more than two months in order to pay his quarterly rent to the landlord. Consequently, over two months, this money might have passed through the hands of a hundred entrepreneurs without essentially delaying the circulation needed within the state.

After all, the landlord's principal rent must be considered as the most necessary and considerable part of the money in circulation. Ready money may always remain in the city if the landlord lives there and the farmer sells all his commodities and buys all the necessary merchandise for his consumption in the countryside in the same city. The farmer will sell there commodities exceeding half the produce of his farm; in the same [181] city he will pay one-third of this produce to the landlord in money, and he will pay the surplus to the merchants or entrepreneurs for the merchandise that is needed for consumption in the countryside. Even here, however, as the farmer sells his commodities in bulk, which then need to be distributed into retail lots, and are then collected again so as to constitute bulk payments to the farmers, the circulation produces the same effect (subject to its rapidity) as if the farmer brought back the money paid for his commodities to the countryside, only to send it back again to the city.

Circulation always consists of the large sums the farmer receives from the sale of his products that are broken up for sale at the retail level, and then collected again to make large payments. This money may be considered [182] as constituting the circulation between the city and the countryside, irrespective of whether some of it leaves the city or remains entirely there. All of the circulation is carried out between the state's inhabitants, and all of them are fed and maintained in every respect through the land's produce and the raw materials of the countryside.

For example, it is true that the wool drawn from the countryside, when made into cloth in the city, is worth four times more than its previous value. But this increase in value, which is the price of the city's workers and manufacturers, is exchanged again for the countryside's produce, which serves to maintain these workers. [183]

4 *Further reflection on the rapidity or slowness of the circulation of money in exchange*

Let us suppose that the farmer pays 1,300 ounces of silver each quarter to the landlord, who each week pays 100 ounces to the baker, the butcher, and so forth, and that these entrepreneurs repay these 100 ounces each week to the farmer, in such a way that the farmer collects on a weekly basis as much money as the landlord spends. Using this assumption, there will be only 100 ounces of silver in continuous circulation, and the other 1,200 ounces will remain on hand, some of it with the landlord and some with the farmer.

[184] But it rarely arises that the landlords spend their rents in a fixed and regular proportion. In London, as soon as the landlord receives his rent, he deposits most of it with a goldsmith or a banker, who lends it at interest, and in consequence this part circulates. Alternatively, this landlord uses a good part of it to purchase several things necessary for the household. Before he obtains rent for the second quarter, he may

perhaps borrow money. Thus the money for the first quarter's rent will circulate in a thousand ways before it is collected and returned to the farmer so as to provide the payment for the second quarter.

When payment for the second quarter is required, the farmer will sell his produce in large amounts, and those who [185] buy his cattle, wheat, hay, and so on will have already earned the price through their retail sales. Thus the first quarter's money will have circulated in the retail channels for nearly three months before it is collected by the retail entrepreneurs, who will give it to the farmer, enabling him to make his payment for the second quarter. It would appear from this that a smaller amount of ready money than we have previously assumed would suffice for circulation in the state.

All exchanges made by book credits do not require very much cash. If a brewer provides a draper with the beer for his family, and if, reciprocally, the draper provides the brewer with the clothes that he needs, all of these determined at the current market price on the delivery day, the only [186] cash that is required between these two traders is the amount that will pay the difference for the greater of the two transactions.

If a merchant in a town sends commodities from the countryside for sale to his correspondent in the city, and if the latter sends back to the former the city's merchandise that is needed for consumption in the countryside, the cash required to conduct this trade—given the annual business between these two entrepreneurs and the mutual confidence that enables them to lodge their goods and merchandise at the respective market prices in their account—will amount only to the balance that one owes to the other at the end of the year. Even then it will be possible to carry forward this amount to a new account for the following year without resorting to using actual money. All the city's entrepreneurs, [187] who are continuously trading with one another, may use this method. These credit exchanges appear to save a great deal of money from circulation, or at least to accelerate its rapidity by making it redundant for the many hands through which it would necessarily have to pass, in the absence of this confidence and this manner of trading on credit. Thus it is easy to understand why it is commonly observed that confidence in trade makes money less scarce.

Goldsmiths and public bankers, whose notes pass in payment like cash, also contribute to the rapidity of circulation, which would be delayed if actual money were needed for all the payments where it suffices to use these notes. Even though these goldsmiths and bankers keep [188] a significant amount of the money they have received in exchange for their notes in reserve, they also put into circulation a considerable quantity of this actual money, as I will later explain when dealing with public banks.

All of these reflections appear to prove that the circulation of a state could be carried out with a lot less actual money than that which I supposed necessary. But the following illustrations appear to counterbalance these and to contribute to the slowing down of this circulation.

First I will note, as I have often intimated, that all the countryside's goods are produced by a labor that may be employed, absolutely speaking, with little or no actual money. But all the cities' or towns' merchandise [189] is made by the work of laborers, who must be paid in actual money. If a house cost 100,000 ounces of silver to build, all of this sum, or at least the greater part of it, must have been paid, directly or indirectly, every week in small amounts to the brickmaker, the masons, the carpenters, and so forth. The expenditure of modest families, who are always the most numerous in a city, is necessarily made with actual money, and in these small exchanges credit, book credits, and notes have no place. The merchants or retail entrepreneurs demand cash for the prices of the goods that they provide, or, if they provide credit to some family for a couple of days, they will demand payment in [190] silver. A carriage builder, who sells a carriage for 400 ounces of silver in notes, will be obliged to convert the notes into actual money to pay for all the materials and all the workers who built his carriage if they worked on credit, or, if he has already paid them in advance, to make a new one. The carriage's sale will make a profit for his business, and he will spend this profit on his family's upkeep. He cannot be content to keep the notes, except when he can put some aside or lend at interest.

The consumption of a state's population is, in a sense, uniquely for food. Accommodation, clothing, furniture, and the like correspond to the food of the workers who provide them, and in the cities all the food and drink must necessarily [191] be paid for with actual money. For urban landlords' families, food is paid for either daily or weekly; wine is paid for either weekly or monthly; hats, stockings, shoes, and the like are normally paid for with actual money; at least these payments correspond to the cash paid to the workers who provided them. All the amounts that are used to make large payments are necessarily divided, distributed, and spread around in small payments corresponding to the subsistence of workers, servants, and so forth, and all these small sums are also necessarily collected and reunited by the smaller entrepreneurs and retailers, who provide for the subsistence of the inhabitants, so as to make large payments when they buy produce from the farmers. [192] A publican collects by pennies and shillings the amounts that he pays to the brewer, and the latter uses them to pay for the grain and the materials that he buys from the countryside. It is impossible to conceive of monetary purchases in a state, such as furniture or merchandise, at a value that does not correspond to the subsistence of those who worked on it.

The circulation in the cities is carried out by entrepreneurs and always corresponds, either directly or indirectly, to the subsistence of servants, workers, and the like. It is inconceivable that it may be carried out at a retail level without actual money. Notes may serve as tokens for large payments for a certain time. But when the time comes to distribute and to spread around the large payments in small transactions, [193] as is always the case sooner or later for circulation in a city, the notes cannot be used for this purpose, and it is necessary to resort to actual money.

Bearing in mind all of the above, all of the orders in a state who are thrifty save and keep some small amounts of cash out of circulation, until they have enough to lend at interest or profit.

Any number of miserly and fearful people bury and hoard cash for periods of time that may be quite lengthy.

Any number of landlords, entrepreneurs, and others always keep some cash in their pockets or safes to meet unforeseen contingencies and so as not to run out of money. If a gentleman remarks that he never [194] had less than 20 louis in his pocket over the course of a year, it may be said that this pocket kept 20 louis out of circulation during the year. No one likes to spend just to the last penny or to have an empty purse. People are happy to receive a new supply of money before paying a debt, even if they already have the money.

Minors' and legal suitors' assets are often deposited as cash and kept out of circulation.

Aside from the large payments that the farmers circulate on a quarterly basis, many others are made between entrepreneurs on the same terms, and others for different maturities between borrowers and moneylenders. All these sums are collected in the retail trade [195] and sooner or later returned to the farmer. But they appear to require a greater amount of actual money for circulation than if these large payments were made at times different from those made when the farmers were paid for their commodities.

There is such a great variety in the different classes of inhabitants in the state, and in the corresponding circulation of actual money, that it appears impossible to be specific or exact with respect to the proportion of money that suffices for circulation. I have produced only as many examples and illustrations as necessary to explain that my supposition is not far from the truth "that the actual money necessary for circulation in a state corresponds almost to the value of a third of all [196] the landlords' annual rents." All other things being equal, more cash is required for circulation when the landlords take a rent amounting to half of the produce or more than a third. A smaller amount of money could suffice when there is great confidence in the banks and in book credits, and also when the rapidity of circulation may be accelerated in other ways. But I will show later that the public banks do not bring as many advantages as is commonly believed. [197]

5

Of the inequality in the circulation of actual money in a state

The city always furnishes many commodities to the countryside, and the landlords who live there must always receive about one-third of the land's produce. Thus the countryside owes more than half of the land's produce to the city. If all of the landlords lived in the city, this debt would always be greater than a half. But, as some of the less important landlords live in the countryside, I presume that the balance, or the debt, which continually returns from the country-side to the city, is equal to one-half of the land's produce [198] and that this balance is paid for in the city by half of the countryside's produce, which is brought there and whose sale price is used to pay this debt.

But all of a state or kingdom's countryside owes a constant balance to the capital, as much for the rent paid to the great landlords who live there as for the state or Crown's taxes, most of which are spent in the capital. All the provincial cities also owe the capital a constant balance, either for the state's property or consumption taxes, or for the different commodities drawn from the capital. It also happens that some indi-viduals and landlords who live in provincial cities spend part of their time [199] in the capital either for their pleasure, or to await the verdict of their cases in final [judicial] appeal, or because they send their chil-dren there to acquire a fashionable education. Consequently, all of these expenditures that are made in the capital are drawn from the pro-vincial cities.

It may therefore be said that all of the state's countryside and cities regularly owe an annual balance or a debt to the capital. But, as all of this is paid in money, it is certain that the provinces must always owe considerable sums to the capital, because the commodities and mer-chandise that the provinces send to the capital are sold there for money, and this money is used to pay the debt or balance in question.

Let us now suppose that the circulation of money is equal in both the provinces and in the capital [200] relative to both the quantity of money and the rapidity of its circulation. The balance will first be sent to the capital in cash, and this will reduce the quantity of money in the provinces while increasing it in the capital. Consequently, the com-modities and merchandise will be more expensive in the capital than in the provinces, due to the greater quantity of money in the capital. The difference in prices between the capital and the provinces must pay for the costs and risks of transport. Otherwise cash will continue to be transported to the capital for the payment of the balance. This state of affairs will last until the difference in prices between the capital and the provinces is equal to the costs and risks of transport. Then the towns' merchants or entrepreneurs will buy [201] the villages' commodities at a low price and will have them transported to the capital to be sold there at a higher price. This difference in prices will necessarily pay for the upkeep of the horses and servants and the profit of the entrepreneur. Otherwise he would close down his businesses.

It follows from this that the prices of commodities of equal quality will always be higher in the countryside that is closer to the capital than that which is further distant, in proportion to the costs and risks of transport. Likewise, the countryside adjacent to seas and rivers that are linked with the capital will draw a proportionately better price for the commodities than those that are distant (all other things being equal), because the costs of water transport are considerably lower than those of land transport. On the other [202] hand, the commodities and small items that are not consumed in the capital, either because they are unsuitable, or because their volume makes them unfit for transport, or because they could perish en route, will be at infinitely cheaper prices in the countryside and distant provinces than in the capital, because the quantity of money in circulation is considerably smaller in the distant provinces.

It is therefore in this way that fresh eggs, game, fresh butter, wood for fuel, and the like will normally sell at a cheaper price in the province of Poitou than in Paris, while wheat, cattle, and horses will be dearer in Paris only to the extent of the difference in costs and risks of sending them and paying tolls for entering the city.

[203] It would be easy to draw an infinite number of similar inductions to justify by experience the necessity of an inequality in the circulation of money in different provinces of a great state or a kingdom, and to show that this inequality is always relative to the balance or the debt owing to the capital.

If we suppose that the balance owing to the capital constitutes one-quarter of the produce of the land of all the state's provinces, the best use that could be made of these lands would be to use those adjoining the city to produce the types of commodities that could not be drawn from distant provinces without a great deal of cost or waste. In effect this is what always happens. The capital's market prices guide the farmers regarding the way to use their lands. They exploit [204] the nearest, when they are suitable, for market gardens, pastures, and so forth.

But manufactures of cloth, linen, lace, and the like should be established in the distant provinces to the extent that this is possible, as should manufactures producing iron, tin, copper tools, and the like in the neighborhood of coal mines or forests, which are otherwise useless because of their distance. In this way it would be possible to send finished goods to the capital at considerably lower transport costs than if the raw materials were sent to be manufactured in the capital, along with the subsistence for the workers employed in producing them. That would save on a vast quantity of horses and freight transporters, which would be better employed for the good of the state: the lands would serve to maintain useful local workers and craftsmen, [205] and the vast number of redundant freight horses could be reduced. Thus the distant lands would yield considerably higher rents to the landlords, and the inequality in circulation between the provinces and the capital could be lessened and better proportioned.

To establish these manufactures, however, it is necessary to have not only considerable encouragement and funds, but also the means to ensure a regular and constant consumption either in the capital city itself, or in certain foreign countries. Exports to these countries may assist the capital city in making payments for merchandise imported from these foreign countries or for the return of silver bullion.

Perfection is not attained immediately once these manufactures [206] are established. The manufactures in question will not succeed if another province has better or cheaper manufactures, or better-located ones close to the capital or near a connecting sea or river, which facilitates their transport. All these circumstances must be examined when establishing a manufacture. I do not propose to deal with them in this essay; I only suggest that, as much as possible, manufactures should be established in the provinces distant from the capital, so as to make them more considerable, and so as to produce there a more equal circulation of money proportional to that of the capital.

For when a distant province, inaccessible [207] by water to the capital or to the sea, has no manufactures and produces only ordinary commodities, it is astonishing the extent to which money is scarce there proportionately to that circulating in the capital, and how little the best lands there produce in taxes and income for the prince and the landlords who live in the capital.

The wines from Provence and Languedoc, sent to the north via the straits of Gibraltar by a long and difficult route, and having passed through the hands of several entrepreneurs, yield very little to their owners in Paris.

However, despite the disadvantages of transport and the distance from the capital or elsewhere, either in the state or in foreign countries, it is necessary that the distant provinces send their commodities, so that the returns from them pay for the balance due to [208] the capital. But if there were works or manufactures to pay this balance, these commodities would be locally consumed, and in this case the population would be much bigger.

When the province pays only the balance with the commodities that yield little in the capital relative to the costs of transport, it is evident that the landlord who lives in the capital gives up the produce of much of his provincial lands to receive little in the capital. This arises from the inequality of money, and this inequality is due to the constant balance that the province owes to the capital.

Currently, if a state or a kingdom that provides all the foreign countries with its own manufacturing products, undertakes [209] so much of this trade that it annually runs a constant external balance, the circulation there will become greater than in foreign countries, money will be more abundant, and, consequently, land and labor will gradually become more expensive there. It follows from this that, as long as these circumstances persist, all the branches of trade of the state in question will exchange a smaller for a greater amount of land and labor with the foreigner.

But if a foreigner lives in the state in question, it will be almost the same situation and the same circumstance for him as it is for the landlord in Paris who has his lands in distant provinces.

Since the creation in 1646 of cloth manufactures and the other works that subsequently followed, France appeared [210] to have traded, at least in part, in the way that I have just discussed. Since the decay of France, England has taken possession of this trade, and all the states appear to be flourishing only by the part of it that they have more or less managed to acquire. All other things being equal, the inequality in the circulation of money in different states constitutes the comparative inequality of power. This inequality in circulation always derives from the balance of foreign trade.

It is easy to judge by what is said in this chapter that Mr. Vauban's estimate of the taxes to be derived from the royal tithe would be neither advantageous nor practicable. It would be fairer to impose a monetary tax on the lands proportional to the landlords' rents. But I must not stray from my subject to show [211] the inconvenience and impossibility of Mr. Vauban's proposal.

6
Of the increase and reduction in the actual quantity of money in a state

If gold or silver mines are discovered in a state, and if considerable quantities of minerals are mined from them, the owner of these mines, the entrepreneurs, and all those who work in them will increase their expenditures proportionately to the wealth and profits that they make. They will also lend sums of money at interest over and above what they need to spend.

All of this money, whether lent or spent, will enter into circulation [212] and will not fail to increase the prices of commodities and merchandise in all the channels of circulation that it enters. The increase in money will bring about an increase in expenditure, and this increase in expenditure will cause an increase in market prices in the peak years of exchange and gradually in the trough years.

Everyone agrees that an abundance of money, or its increase in exchange, raises all prices. This truth has been borne out in practice through the quantity of money brought from America to Europe over the last two centuries.

Mr. Locke presents as a fundamental maxim that market prices are determined by the quantity of commodities and merchandise in proportion to the quantity of money. I have tried [213] to throw light on his idea in the previous chapters: he clearly understood that the abundance of money makes everything dearer, but he has not examined how this happens. The great difficulty of this research is in knowing in what way and in what proportion the increase in money raises prices.

I have already pointed out that an acceleration, or a greater rapidity, in the circulation of money in exchange is, up to a certain point, equivalent to an increase of actual money. I have also pointed out that an increase or reduction in prices in a distant market, either domestic or foreign, influences market prices. On the other hand, money circulates at retail level through such a sizable number of channels that it appears impossible not to lose sight of it, given that, having been amassed [214] into large amounts, it is distributed in the small streams of exchange and that it is gradually accumulated again so as to make large payments. It is necessary, for these operations, to exchange continually gold, silver, and copper coins according to the speed of this exchange. It may also normally be the case that the increase or decrease of actual money in a state is not actually perceived because it flows abroad, or is introduced into the state, by such imperceptible ways and proportions that it is impossible to know precisely the quantity that enters or leaves the state.

We witness all these operations, however, and everyone is directly involved in them. Hence I believe that I may chance some reflections on this matter, although I [215] cannot provide an exact and precise account of them.

I reckon in general that an increase in actual money produces a proportional increase in consumption in a state, which gradually increases prices.

If the increase in actual money comes from a state's gold and silver mines, the mines' owner, the entrepreneurs, the smelters, the refiners, and generally all those who work in them will increase their expenditure in line with their gains. At home they will consume more meat and wine or beer than they used to, and they will become accustomed to having better clothes, finer linen, and more ornate houses and other sought-after commodities. Consequently they [216] will give employment to some craftsmen who hitherto had not as much work and who, for the same reason, will increase their expenditure. All of this increased expenditure on meat, wine, wool, and the like will necessarily reduce the share of other people in the state who are not the initial beneficiaries from the wealth of the mines in question. The bargaining in the market, with the demand for meat, wine, wool, and the like being stronger than usual, will not fail to increase their prices. These high prices will encourage farmers to employ more land to produce them in another year; these same farmers will profit from this price increase and will, like the others, increase their family's expenditure. As a consequence those who suffer first from this dearness and the increase in consumption [217] will be the landlords during the term of their leases, then their servants and all the workers or people on fixed wages on which their families depend. All of them will have to reduce their expenditure in proportion to the new consumption, which will force a large number of them to leave the state to earn their living elsewhere. Some will be laid off by the landlords, and it will happen that the others will ask for an increase in their wages so as to live as before. This is, more or less, the way a sizable increase in money drawn from the mines expands consumption and, in reducing the number of inhabitants, brings about a greater expenditure for those who remain.

If money continues to be drawn from the mines, this abundance of money will increase all prices [218] to the point that not only will the landlords, at the termination of their leases, increase their rents considerably and settle back into their old style of living, increasing proportionally their servants' wages, but the craftsmen and workers will push the price of their articles so high that there will be a considerable profit to be made by importing them from abroad, where they are made more cheaply. This will naturally encourage some to import into the state a large amount of articles made in foreign countries, where they are more cheaply produced. This will gradually destroy the state's craftsmen and manufacturers who, given the high cost of living, will not be able to subsist by working at such low prices.

[219] The money made from the mines will necessarily flow overseas to pay for what is imported when an excessive abundance of money from the mines has reduced the population of a state, accustomed

those who remain to lavish expenditure, increased excessively the prices of the output of land and labor, and ruined the state's manufactures because of the landlords' and mineworkers' recourse to foreign goods. This will imperceptibly impoverish this state and make it, in some manner, dependent on the foreign countries to whom it is obliged to send the money annually as it is drawn from the mines. The great circulation of money, which was general at the start, ceases; poverty and misery follow, and the mines' output appears to be [220] of benefit only to those employed in them, and to the foreigners who profit from them.

This is roughly what has happened to Spain since the discovery of the Indies. As for the Portuguese, since the discovery of gold mines in Brazil, they have almost always used foreign articles and manufactures, and it appears that they work the mines only for the account and advantage of these same foreigners. All the gold and silver mined by these two states do not provide them with more circulation than the others. England and France usually have even more.

Now if the increase of money in the state comes from a balance of foreign trade (that is, exporting articles and manufactures of greater [221] value and in greater quantity than is imported, and consequently receiving the surplus in money), this annual increase in money will enrich a great number of the state's merchants and entrepreneurs, and will give employment to numerous craftsmen and workers who provide the articles that are exported to the country from which the money is drawn. This will gradually increase the industrious inhabitants' consumption, and raise the prices of land and labor. But the industrious people, who are eager to accumulate assets, will not initially increase their expenditure. They will wait until they have accumulated a good sum on which they can earn a guaranteed rate of interest independently of their trade. When a great number of people have acquired considerable fortunes from [222] this money, which regularly and annually enters the state, they are sure to increase their consumption and to raise the price of everything. Although this dearness leads them to greater expenditure, which they had not initially contemplated, they will for the most part continue as long as their capital lasts, given that nothing is easier or more agreeable for families than to increase their expenditure, and nothing is more difficult or more disagreeable for them than to cut back.

If an annual and continuous balance causes a considerable increase of money in a state, it will not fail to increase consumption, raise the price of everything, and even diminish the number of inhabitants, unless an additional [223] amount of commodities is drawn from abroad proportional to the increase in consumption. Moreover, it is normal for states that have acquired a considerable quantity of money to import many things from neighboring countries where money is scarce and consequently everything is cheap. But as money must be sent to pay for this, the balance of trade will be reduced. The cheap price of land and labor in foreign countries where money is scarce will naturally encourage the establishment of manufactures and works there similar to those of the state, but initially they will not be as perfect or as greatly valued.

In this situation the state may subsist with an abundance of money, consume all its produce and even much of the produce of foreign countries, and, over and above all of this, [224] maintain a small balance of foreign trade, or at least keep this balance for many years at par, that is, take as much money from foreign countries in exchange for its articles and manufactures as it is obliged to send to them for the commodities and produce of the land drawn from them. If the state is a maritime one, the ease and cheapness of its shipping for the transport of its articles and manufactures to foreign countries will compensate it in some way for the high cost of labor arising from the excessive abundance of money. In this way this state's articles and manufactures, expensive though they may be there, will sometimes sell in distant foreign countries at lower prices than another state's manufactures [225] where labor is cheaper.

The costs of transport greatly increase the prices of goods exported to distant countries, but these costs are very reasonable in maritime states, where there is regular shipping to all foreign ports, so that ships ready to sail are nearly always found to take all the merchandise entrusted to them at a very reasonable freight charge.

It is not the same in states with less prosperous shipping. There it is necessary to construct ships specifically designed to transport merchandise, which sometimes takes all the profit. Shipping is always expensive there, something that is utterly inimical to trade.

England consumes today [226] not only the greater part of the little it produces, but also much that is produced in other lands, such as silks, wines, fruits, linen in great quantity, etc., while only sending abroad mainly the produce of its mines, its articles, and its manufactures. Moreover, expensive though labor be due to the abundance of money, it still sells its produce to remote countries through the advantage of its shipping, at prices as reasonable as those in France, where these same articles are much cheaper.

The increase in the state's actual quantity of money may also arise, without a balance of trade, through subsidies paid to this state by foreign powers; through the expenses of several ambassadors, or of travelers, tempted to come and stay for some time due to political reasons, [227] or due to curiosity or entertainments to be seen; or through the transfer of the assets and fortunes of some families who, due to the search for religious freedom or other causes, leave their own country to establish themselves in this state. In all of these cases the sums entering the state always raise expenditure and consumption there and consequently increase the prices of all things in the exchange channels through which the money flows.

Let us suppose that, before the quantity of money begins to increase, a quarter of the state's inhabitants daily consume meat, wine, beer, and the like and often provide themselves with clothes, linen, and so forth, but that, once the quantity has begun increasing, a third or a half of the inhabitants consume [228] these same things: the prices of these commodities and merchandises will certainly rise, and the high cost of meat will oblige some of those who formed the original quarter to consume less of it than usual. A man who eats three pounds of meat per day can certainly continue to live on two pounds, but he will feel this cutback, while the other half of the inhabitants, who seldom ate meat before, will scarcely feel it. As I have often suggested, bread will gradually rise in price because of this increase in consumption, but it will be less expensive relative to meat. The increase in the price of meat causes a reduction in consumption for a small section of the population, and so is felt; but the increase in the price of bread reduces the share of

[229] all and accordingly is not felt in the same way. If an additional hundred thousand people come to live in a state with a population of ten million people, their additional consumption of bread will constitute only one pound in a hundred, which will need to be taken from the former population; but when a man consumes 99 pounds of bread rather than 100 pounds, he scarcely feels the cutback.

When meat consumption increases, the farmers expand their pastures to produce more meat, which reduces the quantity of arable land, and consequently the quantity of wheat. Normally the factor that causes the price of meat to rise proportionally more than the price of bread is that the state usually permits [230] the free import of wheat from foreign countries, whereas the import of cattle is absolutely forbidden, as is the case in England, or heavy import duties are imposed, as is done in other states. This is the reason that the rents for English pastures and meadows rise three times more than the rents of arable land when there is an abundance of money.

There is no doubt that the ambassadors, travelers, and families who come to live in the state expand consumption, and that as a result prices increase in all the exchange channels where money is introduced.

As for the subsidies that the state receives from foreign powers, they may be either hoarded due to the state's needs, or put into circulation. If we suppose them to be hoarded, [231] they do not enter into my discussion, for I consider only money in circulation. Hoarded money, plate, church silver, and the like constitute wealth that the state may find useful in great emergencies, but they are of no present utility. If the state puts the subsidies in question into circulation, it can do so only through expenditure, and this will very certainly increase consumption and will raise all prices. The recipient of this money will put it in motion in the principal business of life, which is the sustenance, for either himself or someone else, since everything directly or indirectly relates to this. [232]

7

Continuation of the same topic relating to the increase or reduction of the actual quantity of money in a state

Since gold, silver, and copper have an intrinsic value proportional to the land and labor that enter into their production at the mines, along with their costs of importation or introduction into the states that have no mines, the value of the quantity of money, like that of all other merchandise, is determined by market bargaining against other things.

If England begins for the first time to use gold, silver, and copper in [233] exchange, money will be valued according to the quantity of it in circulation proportionally to its value against all other merchandise and commodities, and this value will be roughly determined by market bargaining. On the basis of these calculations, the landlords and entrepreneurs will fix the daily or annual wages of their servants and laborers in such a fashion that both they and their families may be able to live on the wages that they are given.

Now let us suppose that the ambassadors' and travelers' residence in England has brought into circulation as much money as there was at the start. This money will first pass through the hands of a number of craftsmen, servants, [234] entrepreneurs, and others who will have had some share of the work providing these foreigners with carriages, amusements, etc. The manufacturers, farmers, and other entrepreneurs will feel the benefit of this increase of money, which will accustom a great number of people to far greater expenditure than in the past, something that will consequently increase market prices. Even the children of these entrepreneurs and craftsmen will enter into new expenditures: thanks to such abundance, their fathers will give them some money for their small pleasures, with which they will buy cakes, small patés, etc. This new quantity of money will be distributed in such a way that many who lived without managing any money will be in a position to have some in the current case. Many of the exchanges [235] that were previously facilitated through the granting of credit will now be carried out with cash, and consequently the circulation of money in England will be more rapid than it was at the outset.

I conclude from all of this that the doubling of the quantity of money in a state does not always double the price of commodities and merchandise. A river that flows and twists in its bed will not flow with double the speed when the quantity of water in it is doubled.

The amount of additional expenditure that the quantity of money and its increase introduce into the state will depend on the turn that this money gives to consumption and circulation. Irrespective of the people who obtain this money, it will naturally increase consumption. [236] Consumption, however, will be greater or lesser depending on the circumstances. It will be directed more or less to certain types of commodities or merchandise according to the bent of the money holders. Irrespective of the abundance of money, market prices will increase more for certain types of goods than for others. In England the price of meat could be tripled without the price of wheat increasing by more than a quarter.

In England the importation of wheat from foreign countries is always permitted while that of cattle is forbidden. Given this, no matter how great the actual increase of money in England, the price of wheat can be pushed higher than in other countries only where money is scarce to the extent of the cost and risk associated with [237] importing wheat from these same foreign countries.

It is not the same with cattle prices, which will necessarily be determined by the quantity of money offered for meat in proportion to the quantity of this meat and the number of cattle bred there.

A bullock, weighing eight hundred pounds, sells currently in Poland and Hungary for 2 or 3 ounces of silver, whereas it is usually sold on the London market for more than 40 ounces of silver. However, the bushel of wheat does not sell in London for double the price that it sells for in Poland and Hungary.

The expansion of money increases the price of commodities and merchandise only by the difference in the cost of transport when this transport is permitted. [238] However, in many cases this transport could cost more than a good is worth, so that timber is often redundant in many places. This same cost of transport is the reason that milk, fresh butter, salad, game, etc. cost almost nothing in provinces distant from the capital.

I conclude that an expansion of actual money in a state always produces an increase of consumption and a propensity toward greater expenditure. But the higher prices caused by this money are not found equally across all kinds of commodities and merchandise in proportion to the quantity of this money, except when what is introduced remains in the same channels of circulation as before, that is, unless those who used to pay [239] one ounce of money in the markets are the same, and the only ones who now pay two ounces when the amount of money in circulation is increased to double its weight, which is something that seldom occurs. I conceive that when a large amount of extra money is introduced into a state, the new money brings a new turn to consumption and even to the speed of circulation; however, it is not possible to assess the exact extent.

8

Further reflection on changes in the quantity of money in a state

We have seen that the quantity of money in a state can be expanded through the output of its mines, [240] subsidies from foreign powers, the immigration of foreign families, and the residence of ambassadors and travelers, but, above all, through an annual and regular balance of trade by the export of articles to foreigners so as to draw from them at least a part of the price in gold and silver coins. By this last means a state grows most substantially, particularly when the trade is accompanied and supported by a sizable shipping fleet and a significant domestic production capable of providing the necessary materials for the articles and manufactures that are exported.

The continuation of this trade, however, gradually introduces a great abundance of money and, little by little, expands [241] consumption.

To meet this, a great number of commodities need to be imported from abroad, and this results in part of the annual balance being used to pay for them. On the other hand, the habit of spending pushes up the cost of labor so that the prices of manufactured articles keep rising. It will inevitably happen that some foreign countries will attempt to create the same type of crafts and manufactures and thereby stop buying those of the state in question. Although these new craft establishments and manufactures may initially be rudimentary, they nevertheless delay and ultimately prevent the export of those goods from the neighboring state into their own country, where they may be purchased at a cheaper price.

In this way the state starts to lose some outlets [242] of its profitable trade. Many of the workers and craftsmen, seeing the slowdown in work, emigrate from the state to find more employment in the country with the new manufacture. Despite this reduction in the state's balance of trade, the same former practices involving the importation of various commodities from abroad will continue. The good reputation of the state's crafts and manufactures, and the freighting facilities that provide the means to send them at low cost to distant countries, enable the state to maintain control for many years over the new manufactures that we have discussed, and will even enable it to continue to maintain a small balance of trade or at least to keep it equal. However, if some other maritime state tries to perfect similar articles along with [243] its shipping, it will, through its cheap prices, capture many branches of trade from the state in question. Consequently, this latter state will start to lose its balance of trade and will be obliged every year to send abroad part of its money to pay for the commodities that it imports.

Moreover, even if the state in question manages to maintain a balance of trade alongside its greater abundance of money, it may be reasonably supposed that this abundance will not emerge without producing many wealthy individuals committed to luxury expenditure. They will buy paintings and precious stones from abroad, they will want to have silks and some rare objects, thereby accustoming the state to such luxurious habits that, despite the advantages derived from its [244] ordinary trade, money will annually flow abroad to pay for this same luxury. This will progressively impoverish the state and transform it from a great to a weak power.

When a state has reached its highest level of wealth—I always assume that the comparative wealth of states consists in the respective quantities of money that they possess—it will inevitably fall back into poverty by the ordinary course of things. The excessive quantity of money that, as long as it lasts, constitutes the power of states imperceptibly, but naturally, casts them back into poverty. In consequence it would appear that when a state grows by trade and the abundance of money increases excessively the price of land [245] and labor, the prince or the legislator should put aside money, keep it for unforeseen contingencies, and use all means to delay its circulation, other than by force and bad faith, to prevent its articles from becoming too expensive and to curtail the ill effects of luxury.

But, as it is not easy to find the opportune moment for this, or to know when the quantity of money has become excessive relative to what it should be for the good and for the protection of the state's advantages, the princes and the heads of republics, infrequently concerning themselves with this type of knowledge, are interested in using the facility that they find resulting from the abundance of the state's tax revenues only to expand their power and to insult other states on the most frivolous pretexts. All things [246] considered, perhaps they do not do so badly in working to perpetuate the glory of their reigns and their administrations and in leaving monuments to their power and wealth, since according to the natural course of humanity the state must collapse, and they accelerate only a little its fall. It seems, nevertheless, that they should try to do their utmost while they themselves rule the state to make their power last.

It does not take many years to bring a state to the highest point of its abundance, and it takes even less time for it to plunge into poverty due to the lack of trade and manufactures. Leaving aside the rise and fall of the Venetian Republic, the Hanseatic Towns, Flanders, Brabant, and the Dutch Republic, [247] among others, who have succeeded each other in the profitable branches of trade, it may be said that the power of France started to expand only from 1646, when manufactures were established to produce cloth so as to substitute for those previously imported, until 1684, when a number of Protestant entrepreneurs and craftsmen were driven out of the country. This kingdom has done nothing but decline since this last era.

I know of no better rule to measure the abundance or scarcity of money in circulation than that of the landlords' leases and rents. When lands are rented at a high price it is an indicator that money is abundant in the state. But when it is necessary to rent them at a much lower price, this shows, all other things being equal, that money [248] is scarce. I read in an *État de la France* that an acre of vines, rented in 1660 for 200 livres tournois in hard money near Mantes, and consequently not very far from the capital of France, could not be rented in 1700 above 100 livres tournois of far lighter money, even though, during this interval, the silver brought from the West Indies should have naturally pushed up land prices in Europe.

The author attributes this fall in the rent to inadequate consumption. In effect it appears that he noticed that wine consumption had fallen. But I reckon that he mistook the effect for the cause. The actual cause was a far greater scarcity of money in France, which naturally had the effect of reducing consumption. On the contrary, in this essay I have always suggested that the abundance of [249] money naturally expands consumption and contributes above all things to increase the value of land. When an abundance of money raises commodities to a reasonable price, people are eager to work so as to acquire them, but they have not the same eagerness to acquire commodities or merchandise above that necessary for their upkeep.

It is apparent that every state that has more money in circulation than its neighbors has an advantage over them as long as it maintains this abundance of money.

First, it gives less land and labor than it receives in all branches of trade; as the price of land and labor is everywhere calculated in money, this price is higher in the state where money is the most abundant. Thus the state in question sometimes receives the [250] product of two acres of land in exchange for that of one acre, and the labor of two men in return for one. Because of this abundance of circulating money in London, the work of a single English embroiderer costs more than that of ten Chinese embroiderers, even though the Chinese are superior embroiderers and produce more articles each day. In Europe one marvels as to how the [Asiatic] Indians can subsist by working at such a low price and how the excellent cloth that they send to us costs so little.

Second, where money abounds the state's revenues are more easily collected and raised in comparatively greater amounts; in case of war or dispute, this gives the state the means to gain all sorts of advantages over its [251] adversaries with whom money is scarce.

If two princes make war to rule or conquer a state, with one possessing a great amount of money and the other little, except for many estates that may have a value that is twice greater than all the money of his enemy, the first will be likelier, thanks to monetary inducements, to secure the attachment of his generals and officers than the latter will by giving his [generals and officers] twice the value in land and estates. Grants of land are subject to dispute and revocation and may not be relied on as well as the money that is received. Money may purchase food and the armaments of war, even from the state's enemies. Money may be given as payment for secret services without anyone knowing; lands, commodities, and merchandise [252] could not be used for these purposes, nor, likewise, could jewels or diamonds, because they are easy to recognize. After all, all other things being equal, it appears to me that the comparative power and wealth of states consist in the greater or lesser abundance of money circulating in them, *hic et nunc*.

It remains for me to discuss two other means of expanding the quantity of actual money in circulation in a state. The first is when entrepreneurs and private individuals borrow money on which they pay interest to their foreign correspondents, or when foreigners remit their money to the state to purchase shares or government stocks there. Frequently these amount to considerable sums, which the state has to pay annually in interest to foreigners. These methods [253] of expanding money in the state make money much more abundant there and lower the rate of interest. By means of this money the state's entrepreneurs find the way to borrow more easily, to have people make articles, and to establish manufactures in the hope of profiting from them. The craftsmen and all through whose hands this money passes will not fail to consume more than they would have if they had not been employed by means of this money, which consequently raises the prices of all things as if it belonged to the state. By means of this increase in expenditure or consumption that this money causes, the tax revenues arising from consumption are expanded. The sums lent to the state in this way produce many benefits from it, but [254] their consequences are always onerous and inconvenient. The state has to pay an annual interest to the foreigners, and, aside from this loss, the state finds itself at the mercy of foreigners who can drive it into poverty when it takes their fancy to withdraw their funds. It will indeed certainly happen that they will wish to withdraw them at the very time that the state will have most need of them, such as when preparations are in hand to have a war and a hitch is feared. The interest paid to the foreign state is always considerably greater than the expansion in public revenues that this money causes. These money loans are often seen to shift from one country to another depending on the lenders' confidence about the states to which they are sent. But, truth to tell, it happens most of the time that the states burdened by these loans, on which they have over many [255] years paid high interest rates, fail through bankruptcy in the long term to repay the capital. As soon as distrust sets in, the stocks or public shares fall; the foreign shareholders do not like to withdraw them at a loss and prefer to content themselves with the interest while waiting for confidence to revive, but sometimes it never returns. In states that fall into decay, the principal object of ministers is usually to restore confidence and, by this method, to attract money from foreigners by these types of loans: for unless the government fails to keep good faith and to honor its engagements, the money of the subjects will circulate without interruption. It is the foreigners' money that may expand the quantity of actual money in the state.

[256] But recourse to these borrowings, though creating short-term advantages, ends badly and is but a flash fire. To restore a state that has fallen into decay and has a shortage of ready money, it is necessary to create an annual and regular real balance of trade and to ensure, through shipping, the expansion of articles and manufactures that can always be exported cheaply. Merchants are the first to make fortunes, then the lawyers will appropriate part of it for themselves, and the

prince and the tax farmers will acquire some of it at the expense of both of these and distribute their favors as they please. When money becomes too plentiful in the state, luxury will become prevalent and it will fall into ruin.

[257] Such is roughly the circle experienced by a large state that has funds and an industrious people. An able minister is always in a position to restart another round. It does not take many years to see it implemented and succeed, at least at the beginning, which is the most interesting part. The expansion of the quantity of actual money will be perceived in several ways, which my subject matter does not allow me to examine at present.

As for those states experiencing a shortage of funds, and that can expand only by chance and through current circumstances, it is difficult to find the means to facilitate their growth through trade. There are no ministers who can restore the Venetian and Dutch republics [258] to the former glories from which they have fallen. But irrespective of how much they have fallen, Italy, Spain, France, and England with good management may always be more powerful, by trade alone, providing that each state is independently managed, for if all these states were equally well managed, they would be great only in proportion to their respective funds and to the greater or lesser industry of their people.

The last method that I can conceive to expand the quantity of actual money in circulation in a state is by means of arms and violence. This is often mixed with the others, since there are usually provisions for the maintenance of trading rights [259] and the advantages that can be drawn from them in all peace treaties. The exaction of reparations or the forcing of states to subservience is a certain way to take their money from them. I will not undertake to research the ways of putting this approach into practice. I am content to say that all the nations that flourished in this way have inevitably fallen into ruin, similar to states that flourished through their trade. Using this approach the ancient Romans were more powerful than any other known people. However, these same Romans fell into decay through their taste for luxury before they lost an inch of land in their vast territories, and impoverished themselves through the reduction of actual money that had circulated among them and that their luxury forced [260] out of their great empire into eastern nations.

As long as the luxury of the Romans, which started only after the defeat of Antiochus, king of Asia, toward the year 564 B.C., was limited to the produce and labor of all the vast territories under their rule, the circulation of money kept expanding rather than diminishing. The public controlled all the gold, silver, and copper mines of the empire. They had the gold mines of Asia, Macedonia, and Aquilaea and the rich mines, of both gold and silver, of Spain and many other areas. They had several mints where gold, silver, and copper coinage was struck. The Roman expenditure on all the articles and merchandise that they drew from their vast [261] provinces did not reduce the circulation of actual money, nor did it lessen the amount of paintings, statues, and jewels that they drew from them. Although the patricians spent excessively on food, sometimes paying up to 15,000 ounces of silver for just one fish, all of this did not reduce the quantity of money circulating in Rome, given that the tribute coming from the provinces continually replenished it, without mentioning the amounts that the praetors and governors brought back through their extortions. The amounts annually drawn from the mines continued to expand circulation throughout the reign of Augustus. Luxury, however, was already deeply entrenched, and there was much eagerness not only for all the curiosities produced in the empire itself, but also for Indian jewels, [262] for pepper and spices, and for all the rarities of Arabia. In addition, silks that were not produced with the empire's raw materials started to be sought there. But the money drawn from the mines still surpassed the sums exported outside the empire to purchase all of these goods. Nevertheless, during the reign of Tiberius a scarcity of money was felt: this emperor had hoarded in his treasury 2.7 billion sesterces. He had only to borrow 300 million, mortgaged against his landed estates, to reestablish abundance and circulation. Within less than a year of Tiberius's death, Caligula had spent all that treasure, and at this time the abundance of money in circulation peaked in Rome. The frenzy for luxury continually expanded. At the time of Pliny the Historian [263] at least 100 million sesterces annually left the empire, according to his calculations. This was more than was drawn from the mines. According to Pliny the Younger, the price of land fell by a third or more during the reign of Trajan, and money continued to fall until the time of the emperor Septimus Severus. Money was then so scarce in Rome that this emperor built immense wheat granaries as he was unable to amass sufficiently sizable treasures for his enterprises. Thus, through the loss of its money, the Roman Empire fell into decay before it lost any of its territories. Here is what luxury caused and will always cause in similar circumstances. [264]

9 *Of the interest of money and its causes*

Just as prices are determined through bargaining in markets by the quantity of things offered for sale relative to the quantity of money that is offered for them, or by what is the same thing, the relative number of buyers and sellers, similarly the money rate of interest in a state is determined by the relative number of lenders and borrowers.

Although money acts as a pledge in exchange, it does not multiply itself or produce interest in basic circulation. The introduction of interest appears to have been driven by the needs of mankind. [265] A man who lends his money on good securities or on land mortgages nevertheless runs the risk of the borrower's ill will, or that of expenses, lawsuits, and losses. But when he lends without security, he runs the risk of losing everything. For these reasons needy people must, at the beginning, have tempted lenders by the lure of profit. This profit must have been proportionate to the needs of the borrowers and to the fear and greed of the lenders. This appears to me to be the origin of interest. But its continued use in states appears to be based on the profits that entrepreneurs can make from it.

Assisted by human labor, land naturally produces 4, 10, 20, 50, 100, and 150 [266] times the amount of wheat that is sown on it, according to the fertility of the soil and the inhabitants' industriousness. It multiplies fruit and cattle. The farmer who works it usually has two-thirds of the produce, of which one-third pays for his expenses and upkeep and the remaining third accrues to him as the profit of his business.

If the farmer has enough funds to conduct his business, if he has all the necessary tools and instruments, along with horses for tillage, cattle to make the land pay, and so forth, he will take for himself one-third of the farm's produce, if all expenses are covered. But if a skillful laborer, who is living on a daily wage and has no funds, can find someone willing to lend him some funds or money to buy one, he will be in a position to give this lender all of the [267] third rent, that is, the third of the produce of a farm where he will become the farmer or the entrepreneur. He will, however, believe his situation to be better than his former one, given that he can provide for his upkeep with the second rent and become a master instead of the servant that he was. If he can slowly amass some small funds, through his savings and by depriving himself of some of his necessities, he will have less to borrow each year and will eventually be able to keep the third rent for himself.

If this new entrepreneur is able to buy wheat or cattle on credit, to be repaid in the long term when he is in a position to sell his farm's produce, he will not mind paying a higher price for it than the market price for ready money. This approach will be the same as if he [268] borrowed cash to buy wheat, paying interest on the difference between the current price and the future price. But whether he borrows either cash or merchandise, he needs to have enough left on which to live from his business; otherwise he will become bankrupt. Because of this risk he will be asked to pay 20 to 30 percent in profit or interest on the quantity of money or on the value of the articles or merchandise that will be lent to him.

On the other hand, a master hatter who has funds to manage his hat business—namely, to rent a house, buy beaver, wool, dye, or the like, or to pay the weekly subsistence of his workers—not only must provide for his own upkeep from this business, [269] but additionally must make a profit similar to that of the farmer who keeps the third part for himself. This upkeep and likewise this profit must come from the sale of the hats, the price of which should cover not only the materials, but also the upkeep of the hatter and of his workers, and also the profit in question.

But a skilled journeyman hatter without funds can carry out the same business by borrowing money and materials and abandoning his profit to anyone who will lend money to him, or to anyone who will provide him with beaver, wool, or the like, whom he will pay only in the long term when his hats are sold. If the lender, on the maturity of his bills, requests his capital, or if the wool merchant and the other lenders [270] no longer wish to rely on him, he will have to give up his business, in which case he will perhaps prefer to go bankrupt. But if he is wise and industrious, he may be able to show his creditors that he has in cash and hats near to the value of the capital that he borrowed, and they will probably prefer to continue to rely on him and to be content for the present with their interest or with the profit. In this way he will continue, and perhaps he will slowly accumulate some capital by cutting back on his necessities. With this assistance, he will have less to borrow each year, and when he has accumulated a sufficient fund to conduct his business, which will always be proportional to his sales, the profit will accrue solely to him, and he will become rich as long as he does not increase his expenditure.

It is appropriate to note that [271] the upkeep of such a manufacturer is small relative to the amounts that he borrows for his business or to the materials that are entrusted to him. Consequently the lenders do not run a big risk of losing their capital if he is an honest and industrious man. Yet, as it is highly possible that he may not be, the lender will always demand from him a profit or interest of 20 to 30 percent of the value of the loan. Even then it may be only those who have a good opinion of him who will trust him. The same illustrations may be given in relation to all the masters, craftsmen, manufacturers, and other entrepreneurs in the state who manage businesses whose funds considerably surpass the value of their annual upkeep.

But if a Parisian water carrier [272] establishes himself as a self-employed entrepreneur, all the funds that he requires will be the price of two buckets, which he may buy for an ounce of silver, after which all that he earns is profit. If through his labor he annually earns 50 ounces of silver, the amount of his funds or borrowing relative to his profit will be one to fifty. That is, he will earn 5,000 percent, whereas the hatter will earn only 50 percent and will even be obliged to pay 20 to 30 percent of it to the lender.

A moneylender, however, will greatly prefer to lend 1,000 ounces of silver to a hatter at 20 percent interest than to lend 1,000 ounces to 1,000 water carriers at 500 percent interest. The water carriers will quickly spend for their upkeep not only [273] the money that they earn by their daily labor, but also all that is lent to them. These capitals lent to them are small relative to the amount that is necessary for their upkeep; irrespective of the amount of work they carry out, they can easily spend all that they earn. Therefore, it is hardly possible to determine the profits of these small entrepreneurs. It could be said that if a water carrier, by hard work, earned 100 ounces of silver annually, he would certainly be said to have increased five or even ten thousand times the value of the buckets that constitute the funds of his business. As he may spend the 100 ounces just as easily as the 50 ounces on his upkeep, however, it is only through learning about the expenditure on his upkeep that it is possible to estimate his clear profit.

[274] Entrepreneurs' subsistence and upkeep must always be deducted before their profit is determined. This has been done with respect to the examples of the farmer and the hatter, but it can hardly be determined for the smallest entrepreneurs, who, if they are in debt, for the most part become bankrupt.

It is usual for the London brewers to lend a few barrels of beer to alehouse entrepreneurs, and when the latter pay for the first barrels they continue to be lent the others. If the consumption of these alehouses grows, the brewers sometimes make a profit of 500 percent annually, and I have heard it said that the big brewers are enriched when no more than half of the alehouses become [275] bankrupt during the year.

All the state's merchants routinely lend merchandise or commodities to retailers for a time, and they proportion their rate of profit, or their interest, to that of their risk. The greater the cost of the borrower's upkeep, the greater the risk for the lender. For if the borrower or retailer does not have rapid sales in his small business, he will quickly be ruined and will spend all that he has borrowed for his upkeep and consequently will be obliged to go into bankruptcy.

The fishwives who buy fish in London's Billingsgate to resell it in other areas of the city normally pay by means of a contract drawn up by an expert scrivener [276] at 1 shilling per guinea, or by 21 shillings of interest each week. This amounts to 260 percent per year. The female hucksters of the Halles in Paris, whose businesses are less considerable, pay 5 sols per week in interest on an écu of 3 livres, which is greater than 430 percent annually. However, few lenders make a fortune from such high rates of interest.

These high interest rates are not only permitted, but are in a way useful and necessary for a state. Those who buy the fish in the streets pay for these high rates of interest through their increased prices. This is convenient for them, and thus they do not feel the loss. Similarly, a craftsman who drinks two pints of beer and pays a price for them that brings the brewer [277] 500 percent profit enjoys this convenience and does not feel the loss involved in such a small transaction.

The Casuists, who hardly appear to be suited to judge the nature of interest and matters of trade, conceived a term (*damnum emergens*), reluctant though they were to approve of these high rates of interest. Rather than upsetting the custom and convenience of society, they consented and permitted those who lent at a great risk to charge proportionally higher rates of interest. These were without limit because they would have been at a loss to find any that were certain, since everything really depends on the lenders' apprehension and the borrowers' needs.

Maritime merchants are praised when they can create profit in their business, [278] even though it may be 10,000 percent, and furthermore, whatever their profit, I have not heard it said that the Casuists criminalized wholesalers for selling commodities and merchandise on credit to smaller retailers. They are, or appear to be, a little more scrupulous concerning money loans, even though they are basically the same thing. Nevertheless, they still tolerate these loans through a distinction (*lucrum cessans*) of their own conception. I believe that this means that a man who has usually been making 500 percent on his money in trade may stipulate this profit when he lends it to another. Nothing is more entertaining than the multiplicity of civil and church laws made in every century relating to the subject of the interest rate, always [279] uselessly and always by philosophers ignorant of trade.

It appears from these examples and inductions that there are many classes and channels of interest or profit in a state. Interest, because it is proportional to the greatest risk, is always the highest for the lowest classes. It falls from class to class up to the highest, which is that of the rich and reputedly solvent merchants. The interest stipulated for this class is that known as the state's current rate of interest, and it differs little from the interest sought on land mortgages. A solvent and reputable merchant's bill is as attractive as a land deed, at least in the short term, since the possibility of a lawsuit or a dispute about the mortgage counterbalances [280] the possibility of the merchant's bankruptcy.

If there were no entrepreneurs in the state who could make a profit on the money or the merchandise that they borrowed, the use of interest would probably be less frequent than is seen. Only the foolish and the prodigal would make loans. But accustomed as people are to making use of entrepreneurs, there is a continual source for loans and consequently for interest. It is the entrepreneurs who cultivate the land, the entrepreneurs who provide bread, meat, clothes, and so on to all of the city's inhabitants. Those who are paid workers of these entrepreneurs also seek to establish themselves as entrepreneurs in emulation of each other. The multiplicity [281] of entrepreneurs is even greater among the Chinese, and as they all are intelligent and have a true genius for business and a considerable application in carrying it out, there are as many entrepreneurs among them as there are those who work at fixed wages among us; they even provide meals for workers in the fields. It is perhaps this multiplicity of small entrepreneurs and others from class to class, who find the means to make a great deal through consumption without it being detrimental to consumers, that keeps the rate of interest for the highest class at 30 percent while it scarcely ever goes above 5 percent for us in Europe. In Athens at the time of Solon, the interest rate was at 18 percent. In the Roman Republic it was most frequently at 12 percent, [282] but it was also seen at 48 percent, at 20 percent, at 8 percent, and at its lowest at 4 percent. It was never so freely low as toward the end of the republic and under Augustus after the conquest of Egypt. The emperors Antoninus and Alexander Severus reduced the rate of interest to only 4 percent when lending public money against land mortgages.

IO
AND LAST

The causes of the increase and decrease of the interest rate on money in a state

It is a common idea, accepted by all who have written on trade, that the increase [283] in the quantity of actual money in a state lowers the rate of interest there, because when money is abundant it is far easier to find money to borrow. This idea is not always true or reasonable. For proof of this it is necessary only to remember that in the year 1720 nearly all the money in England was brought to London and that, even above this, the amount of notes issued there accelerated the movement of money in an extraordinary way. However, this abundance of money and circulation, instead of reducing the current rate of interest, which had been at 5 percent, served only to increase the rate, which was pushed up to 50 and 60 percent. The principles and causes of interest [284] that I established in the preceding chapter make it easy to account for this increase in the rate of interest. Here it is: everyone became an entrepreneur during the South Sea System and sought to borrow money to buy shares, expecting to make an immense profit through which it would be easy to pay this high rate of interest.

If the abundance of money in the state is caused by moneylenders, it will undoubtedly lower the current interest rate by the increase in the number of lenders; but if it is caused by an increase in expenditure it will have the opposite effect. It will push up the rate of interest through the expansion in the number of entrepreneurs who will have work arising from this increased expenditure, and who will need to borrow at different interest rates to supply their business.

[285] The abundance or scarcity of money in a state always raises or

lowers the prices of everything in market bargaining without having any necessary relationship with the rate of interest, which may very well be high in states where there is an abundance of money and low in those where money is scarcer: high where everything is expensive and low where everything is cheap; high in London and low in Genoa.

The rate of interest fluctuates every day through simple rumors that tend to reduce or increase the lenders' confidence, without influencing the prices of things in exchange.

The most regular cause of a state's high rate of interest is the great expenditure of nobles and landlords or of other rich people. Entrepreneurs and master craftsmen [286] customarily supply great houses with all their different types of expenditure. These entrepreneurs nearly always need to borrow money to supply them. The nobility doubly contribute to raising the interest rate when they spend their income in advance and borrow money.

On the contrary, when the country's nobility live frugally and buy at first hand all that they can, procuring through their servants many things that do not pass through the entrepreneurs' hands, they reduce the profits and number of entrepreneurs in the state and consequently the number of borrowers along with the rate of interest, because these types of entrepreneurs, working with their own funds, borrow [287] the least amount possible and, satisfied with a small profit, prevent those who have no funds from intruding into businesses through borrowing. This is currently the situation in the Dutch and Genoese republics, where the rate of interest is sometimes at 2 percent and lower still for the highest class, whereas in Germany, Poland, France, Spain, England, and other states, the ease and expenditure of the nobles and landlords always keep the entrepreneurs and master craftsmen in the habit of sizable profits, and the consequence is that they have the means to pay a high interest rate and even more when they import everything from abroad, involving higher risks in businesses.

The rate of interest is increased for two reasons when the prince or the state is involved in [288] substantial expenditures such as those that arise when involved in war: the first is that this [substantial expenditure] multiplies the number of entrepreneurs for several new war-provisioning businesses and hence increases borrowing. The second relates to the very great risk that war inevitably brings.

On the contrary, when the war is over, the risks are reduced, the number of entrepreneurs falls, and even the war-provisioning entrepreneurs, shutting down their businesses, reduce their expenditures and become moneylenders through the money they have earned. In this situation, if the prince or the state offers to repay part of its debts, the rate of interest will be greatly reduced; and this will have an even greater impact if the state can really pay part of the debt [289] without further borrowing, because the repayments increase the number of lenders in the highest-interest class, and this will in turn influence the habits of the other classes.

When the abundance of money in a state arises from a continual balance of trade, this money will first pass through the entrepreneurs' hands, and although it expands consumption, it does not fail to lower the rate of interest, because most entrepreneurs then acquire sufficient funds to conduct their trade without money, and even become lenders of the sums that they earned over and above that required to conduct their trade. If there is an insufficiency of big-spending nobles and rich people in the state, then, in [290] these circumstances, the abundance of money will certainly reduce the rate of interest, as well as increase the prices of commodities and merchandise in exchange. This is what normally happens in the republics in which funds are scarce, the estates are small, and the only path to wealth is through foreign trade. But in the states that have considerable funds and owners of large estates, the money brought in through foreign trade increases their rents and gives them the means to spend heavily, thereby providing for the upkeep of many entrepreneurs and craftsmen beyond those who are involved in foreign trade. Despite the abundance of money, this always ensures a high interest rate.

When the nobility and landlords [291] ruin themselves through their extravagant expenditure, the moneylenders who have mortgages on their land often take over the absolute ownership of them. It may well happen in the state that the lenders become creditors for a great deal more money than is in circulation. In this case, they may be regarded as the proxy owners of the land and of the commodities mortgaged for their security. If this is not the case, they will lose their capital through bankruptcies.

Similarly, shareholders and the holders of public debt may be considered proxy owners of the state's revenues that are stipulated for making interest payments. But if the legislature was forced, due to the needs of the state, to employ its revenues for other uses, the [292] shareholders, or holders of public debt, would lose everything without the money that circulates in the state being reduced by a single farthing.

If the prince or the state's administrators wish to regulate legally the current rate of interest, it will be necessary to regulate it on the basis of the current market rate for the highest class or thereabouts. Otherwise the law will be useless, because the contracting parties, governed by market bargaining, or the current rate determined by the proportion of lenders to borrowers, will enter into secret agreements, and this legal constraint will serve only to disturb trade and to raise the rate of interest rather than fix it. In times past, the Romans, having initiated several laws to restrict the rate of interest, introduced another law that banned [293] absolutely the lending of money. This law had no more success than its predecessors. The Justinian law restraining the patricians from taking more than 4 percent, those of a lesser class 6 percent, and traders 8 percent, was equally ridiculous and unjust, given that the making of profits of 50 to 100 percent in all sorts of businesses was not forbidden.

If it is permissible and reasonable for a landlord to let a farm at a high rent to an impoverished farmer at the risk of losing all the yearly rent, it would appear that the lender should be permitted to lend his money to a needy borrower at the risk of losing not only his interest or profit but also his capital, and to stipulate any interest rate to which the other will voluntarily [294] agree. It is true that loans of this nature make those people wretched who, losing both the capital as well as the interest, are less capable of recovering than the farmer who does not take away the land. But the bankruptcy laws being sufficiently favorable to the debtors to allow them to start again, it appears that the interest rate laws should always be adjusted to the market rates, as is the case in Holland.

The current market rates of interest in a state appear to serve as the basis and rule in determining the purchase price of land. If the current interest rate is 5 percent, which corresponds to twenty years' purchase, the price of land should be the same. But as the ownership of land gives a status and a [295] certain power in the state, it happens that when the rate of interest is equivalent to twenty years' purchasing power, the price of the land is at twenty-four years' or twenty-five years' purchase, even though the mortgages on these same lands are scarcely greater than the current rate of interest.

After all, the price of land, as is the case for all prices, naturally settles itself by the proportion of sellers and buyers, etc. For example, there will be many more purchasers in London than in the provinces, and as these purchasers who live in the capital will prefer to buy lands in their neighborhood rather than in the distant provinces, they will prefer to buy neighboring land at thirty or thirty-five years' purchase than distant lands at twenty-five years' or [296] twenty-two years' purchase. It is unnecessary to note here that convenience factors often influence the price of land because they do not invalidate our explanations of the nature of interest.

End of the second part.

Part 3

I   *Of foreign trade*

When, in foreign trade, a state exchanges a small product of land against a greater one, it appears to have the advantage in this trade, [298] and if money circulates more abundantly there than abroad, it will always exchange a smaller product of land against a greater one.

When the state exchanges labor against the product of foreign land, it appears to have the advantage in this trade, since its people are maintained at the foreigner's expense.

When a state exchanges its product conjointly with its labor against a greater foreign product conjointly with an equal or greater amount of labor, it again appears to have the advantage in this trade.

If the Parisian ladies annually consume Brussels lace worth 100,000 ounces of silver, a quarter acre of Brabant land that will produce [299] 150 pounds weight of flax to be worked into fine lace in Brussels will correspond to this amount. The annual labor of about two thousand people in Brabant will be required for all the manufacturing constituents from the sowing of the flax to the ultimate refinement of the lace. The Brussels lace merchant or entrepreneur will make advance payments. He will, directly or indirectly, pay all the spinners and lacewomen along with the proportion of the labor of those who make their tools. All those who have part of the work will buy, either directly or indirectly, their maintenance from the Brabant farmer, who pays in part his landlord's rent. If, in this economy, the produce of the land required for the upkeep of these two thousand people, as well as that of their families who in part subsist on it, is calculated at three acres [300] per head, then six thousand acres of Brabant land will be used for the upkeep of those who have worked on the lace, at the expense of the Parisian ladies who will buy and wear this lace.

The Parisian ladies will pay the 100,000 ounces of silver, each one according to the quantity she purchases. All of this money, minus the costs of remitting it, must be sent in specie to Brussels. The Brussels entrepreneur will need to find therein not only the payment for all his advances and the interest on the money that he may have borrowed, but, additionally, a profit from his business for the upkeep of his family. If the price paid for the lace by the ladies does not [301] cover all the costs and profits in general, there will be no encouragement for this business, and the entrepreneurs will give it up or will become bankrupt. But as we have assumed that this manufacture is maintained, it is necessary for the prices paid by the Parisian ladies to cover all the expenses and for the 100,000 ounces of silver to be sent to Brussels, unless the people in Brabant acquire something from France to compensate for it.

But if the people in Brabant like champagne and annually consume the value of 100,000 ounces of silver of it, the wine account will offset that for the lace, and the balance of trade, relative to these two branches, will be equal. The offsetting of accounts and circulation will be [302] carried out through the intermediation of the entrepreneurs and of the bankers who will be involved in it on either side.

The Parisian ladies will pay 100,000 ounces of silver to whomever sells and delivers the lace to them. The latter will pay this amount to the banker in return for one or more bills of exchange drawn on his Brussels correspondent. This banker will remit the money to the Champagne wine merchants, who have 100,000 ounces of silver in Brussels and who will give him their bills of exchange for the same value drawn on him by his Brussels correspondent. Thus the 100,000 ounces paid for the champagne in Brussels will offset the 100,000 ounces paid for the lace in Paris. By means of this the trouble of transporting to Brussels the silver received in Paris, and to Paris the silver received in Brussels, [303] will be avoided. This clearing of accounts is carried out through bills of exchange, the nature of which I will attempt to explain in the next chapter.

This example, however, shows that the 100,000 ounces that the Parisian ladies paid for the lace comes into the hands of the merchants who send the champagne to Brussels, and that the 100,000 ounces that the champagne consumers pay for this wine in Brussels falls into the hands of the entrepreneurs or lace merchants. On each side the entrepreneurs distribute this money to those who work for them either on the wines or on the lace.

It is clear from this example that the Parisian ladies support and maintain all those who [304] work on the lace in Brabant and that they cause the money to circulate there. It is equally clear that the champagne consumers in Brussels support and maintain not only all the wine producers in Champagne, but also all the others involved in the production as well as the cartwrights, farriers, carriers, etc., involved in the transport along with the horses that they use. But they also pay for the value of the produce of the land for the wine, and they cause money to be circulated in Champagne.

This circulation or this trade in Champagne, however, which creates such a stir, and which provides a living for the wine producer, the farmer, the cartwright, the farrier, and the carrier, and which pays exactly the rent of the vineyard owner as well as that of the owner of the pastures that [305] are used to feed the carthorses is, in the present case, an onerous and inconvenient trade for France when its effects are considered.

If a hogshead of wine sells in Brussels for 60 ounces of silver, and if it is assumed that an acre produces four hogsheads, it is necessary to send the produce of 4,166½ acres of land to equate with 100,000 ounces of silver, and it is necessary to employ about two thousand acres of pastures and lands to have the hay and oats eaten by the carthorses, using them solely for this work during the year. Hence the subsistence arising from about six thousand acres of land is taken from French people, and that of the people in Brabant is increased by more than four thousand acres, [306] since the champagne that they drink saves more than four thousand acres that they would probably have used to produce beer as their drink, if they did not drink wine. The lace used to pay all of this, however, costs the people of Brabant only a quarter of an acre of flax. In consequence with the work of only one acre of land, the people of Brabant pay the French for more than sixteen thousand acres' produce, while working less. They profit from an increase of subsistence, while they give in return only a luxury article, which produces no real advantage for France because the lace is worn and cast off there, after which it is impossible to exchange it for something useful. Following the rule of intrinsic values, the land used in Champagne to produce [307] wine, that used for the upkeep of the wine producers, the coopers, the cartwrights, the farriers, the carriers, the carthorses, and so forth, should be equal to the land used in Brabant for the growing of flax and to that needed for the upkeep of the spinners, lace makers, and all those who had some part in the manufacture of the lace.

But if money is more abundant in circulation in Brabant than in Champagne, the land and the labor will be more expensive there, and consequently, as a result of the valuations that are made on both sides in silver, the French will lose even more.

This example shows a branch of trade that strengthens the foreigner, reduces the state's population, and, without [308] causing any actual money to leave it, weakens this same state. I have chosen this example to illustrate better how a state may be the dupe of another in trade, and to better predict the true effects of foreign trade. By examining the actual results of each specific branch of trade, the effects of foreign trade can be predicted in a useful way, a knowledge that cannot be deduced from mere generalities.

It will always be found proven by specific cases that all manufacturing exports are beneficial to the state, because in this instance the foreigner always pays for and maintains workers useful to the state, and that the best returns or payments taken in are those made in specie [309] and, in default of specie, in the produce of foreign land necessitating the smallest amount of labor. Through recourse to these methods of trading, states with very few land products are often seen to maintain a great number of people at the foreigner's expense, and large states to support their people in greater ease and abundance.

But given that large states have no need to increase the number of their inhabitants, it suffices to provide greater comfort and ease to their inhabitants from the raw produce of the state and to increase the state's forces for its defense and security. To attain this through foreign trade, the state's exports of articles and manufactures need to be greatly encouraged, so as to gain from them as much gold and silver [310] in bullion as is possible. If, as a result of bumper harvests, it so happened that the state had a surplus of products above the usual annual consumption, it would be advantageous to encourage their export abroad in return for their value in gold and silver. These metals do not decay or dissipate like other products of the land, and with gold and silver it is always possible to import into the state all that is lacking there.

It would be disadvantageous, however, for the state to be accustomed to exporting great quantities of its raw produce annually in return for foreign-manufactured imports. This would weaken and reduce both the population and the armed forces of the state simultaneously.

But I have no intention [311] of outlining in detail the branches of trade that should be encouraged for the good of the state. It is enough to point out that the importation of money should always be the objective.

The expansion of the quantity of money circulating in a state gives it great advantages in foreign trade so long as this abundance of money is maintained. Through it the state always exchanges a smaller amount of product and labor against a greater one. Taxes are easily raised, and it has no difficulty in finding money in cases of public need.

It is true that the continuation of the monetary expansion will in time cause, through its abundance, a rise in the price of land and labor in the state. In the long run the articles and manufactures [312] will cost so much that foreigners will cease, little by little, to buy them and will become accustomed to purchasing them elsewhere at a better price. This will gradually destroy the state's production and manufactures. The same cause that will increase the landlords' rents—namely, the abundance of money—will accustom them to import many articles from abroad, where they will buy them cheaply. These are natural consequences. The wealth the state acquires through trade, labor, and thrift will gradually push it into luxury. States that rise through trade inevitably fall afterward. Certain measures could be put into practice to arrest this decline, but these are scarcely ever tried. It is always true, however, that the state that has an actual [313] balance of trade and an abundance of money always appears to be powerful, and is so in effect as long as this abundance lasts.

An infinite number of illustrations might be given to justify these ideas on foreign trade and the advantages of an abundance of money. It is astonishing to see the disproportion in the circulation of money in

England and in China. Despite the costs of an eighteen-month sea trip, [East] Indian manufactured goods such as silks, printed calicoes, muslins, and the like are at a very low price in England, which could pay for them with a thirtieth part of its articles and manufactures if the [East] Indians wished to purchase them. But they are not so foolish as to pay extravagant prices for our products, given that they are superior workers to us and produce at an infinitely cheaper [314] price. Therefore they sell their manufactures only for the ready money that we annually bring them, which increases their wealth and reduces our own. The [East] Indian manufactures bought in Europe only reduce our money and the work of our own manufactures.

An American who sells beaver skins to a European is rightly surprised to learn that woolen hats are as good to wear as those made of beaver, and that all the difference, occasioned by such a long sea trip, arises only in the imaginations of those who find beaver hats lighter and more pleasant to the eye and touch. As articles of iron, steel, and the like, however, rather than money, are usually used to pay the Americans for these beaver skins, [315] it is a trade that is not prejudicial to Europe, all the more so since it supports workers and particularly sailors, who are very useful when needed by the state, whereas the trade involving East Indian manufactures removes money and reduces the number of European workers.

It must be acknowledged that the East Indian trade is advantageous to the Dutch Republic, which forces the loss on the rest of Europe by selling the spices and manufactures in Germany, Italy, Spain, and the New World, which more than reimburse it for all the money that it sends to the Indies. It is even useful for Holland to dress its women and many of its inhabitants with [East] Indian manufactures [316] rather than with English or French fabrics. It is of greater benefit for the Dutch to enrich the [East] Indians than their neighbors, who might profit from it to oppress them. Moreover, they sell their own home-produced cloth and small manufactures more expensively to the rest of Europe than what they pay for the Indian manufactures that are domestically consumed.

On this issue England and France would be wrong to imitate the

Dutch. These kingdoms have the domestic means of clothing their women, and, although their fabrics are more expensive than those of the [East] Indian manufactures, they must prevent their inhabitants from wearing foreign fabrics. They cannot permit the scaling down of their own articles and manufactures, or become dependent on foreigners, [317] let alone allow their money to be taken away for this.

But since the Dutch find the means to sell [East] Indian merchandise in the other European states, the English and the French should do the same, to either reduce Dutch naval strength or increase their own, and above all so as not to have to depend on the Dutch in the areas of consumption that an inapposite fad made fashionable in these kingdoms. It is clearly disadvantageous to allow the wearing of [East] Indian fabrics in European kingdoms that have their own materials to clothe their populations.

Just as it is disadvantageous for a state to encourage foreign manufactures, it is also disadvantageous to encourage foreign shipping. [318] When a state exports its articles and its manufactures, it derives the full advantage if it transports them with its own shipping. In this way it maintains a good number of sailors, who are as useful to the state as workers. But if it leaves the transportation to foreign ships, it strengthens foreign shipping and diminishes its own.

Shipping is an essential element of foreign trade. In the whole of Europe it is the Dutch who build the cheapest ships. In addition to the [advantage of] their rivers, on which timber is floated down to them, the neighboring northern areas provide them with cheaper masts, timber, tar, ropes, and so on. Their saw windmills facilitate this work. Further, they sail with smaller crews, and their sailors [319] live very cheaply. The labor of eighty men a day can be saved by one of their windmills for sawing wood.

Due to these advantages, they would be the only sea carriers in Europe if the cheapest market was always sought. Further, if they had enough of their own raw materials to create an extensive trade, they would undoubtedly possess the most flourishing merchant marine in Europe. But their sizable number of sailors is not sufficient to create naval superiority for them without the interior strength of the state.

Even if the state had significant revenues to build and arm warships they would not do so: they would profit in every way from the extended market.

To prevent them from increasing their maritime advantage through their lower costs at its expense, England has forbidden [320] all nations from importing into it all merchandise that is not domestically produced. By means of this the English have strengthened their own merchant marine because the Dutch have been unable to act as carriers into England. Even though English sea freight is more expensive than that of the Dutch, the wealth of their overseas cargoes reduces these costs considerably.

France and Spain are clearly maritime states that have a rich produce that is sent to the north, from whence commodities and merchandise are brought to them. It is not surprising that their merchant marine is small relative to their produce and the extent of their seaboard, because they rely on foreign ships to transport all that they import from the north, and to come and take the commodities that they export to the northern countries. [321]

From a policy perspective these states, France and Spain, do not consider the conditions in which they could make trade a source of profit. Most of the French and Spanish traders involved in foreign trade are agents or clerks of foreign traders rather than entrepreneurs managing this trade with their own funds.

It is true that the northern states, through their situation and proximity to countries that produce all that is necessary for the construction of ships, are in a better position to transport everything at a lower price than would be the case of France or Spain. But if these two kingdoms took measures to strengthen their shipping, this obstacle would not stop them. England has in part [322] for a long time shown them what they might achieve by its example. They have, both at home and in their colonies, all that is necessary to build ships, or at least it would not be difficult there to have them built. An infinity of measures might be taken to establish a successful policy, if the legislature or the administration would agree with it. My subject does not allow me in this essay to examine the detail of these policies. I will limit myself to saying that it is almost impossible for the prince to maintain a flourishing navy, without expenses that would be capable of destroying the state's treasury, in the countries where trade does not continually support a considerable number of ships and sailors.

I will conclude, then, by noting that foreign trade is the most crucial for [323] strengthening or reducing a state's power; that domestic trade is not of similar policy significance; and that foreign trade is only half supported when insufficient attention is given to increasing and maintaining sizable merchants who are natives of the country, ships, sailors, workers, and manufactures. Above all, attention must be paid to maintaining a balance against the foreigners.

2 *Of the exchanges and their nature*

Within the city of Paris it usually costs 5 sols to carry a bag of 1,000 livres from one house [324] to another. If it were necessary to carry it from the Faubourg Saint Antoine to the Invalides it would cost more than double this, and if there were no generally trustworthy money porters it would cost even more. If robbers frequented the roads the money would be sent in large amounts with an escort, involving further expenses. If someone took charge of the transport at his own costs and risk, he would charge for this transport in proportion to the costs and the risk. This explains why the transportation expenses from Rouen to Paris and from Paris to Rouen usually cost 50 sols per bag of 1,000 livres, which in banking parlance is ¼ percent. The bankers usually send the money in double barrels, which the robbers can scarcely carry because of the iron and the weight, [325] and as there are always carriers on this route, the expenses are small for the big sums that are sent in either direction.

If the city of Châlons sur Marne annually pays the king's tax receiver 10,000 ounces of silver on the one hand, and if, on the other hand, the wine merchants of Châlons and its surrounding areas, through their correspondents, sell in Paris champagne to the value of

10,000 ounces of silver, and if the ounce of silver is valued in trade at 5 livres, the sum of 10,000 ounces in question will be called 50,000 livres in both Paris and Châlons.

In this example the tax receiver has 50,000 livres to send to Paris, and the Châlons wine merchants' agents have 50,000 [326] to send to Châlons. This double transaction, or transport, may be avoided by an offset, or, as it is called, by bills of exchange, if the parties agree and arrange it.

Assuming that each of the agents for the Châlons wine merchants brings his respective part of the 50,000 livres to the cashier of the tax farms in Paris, he will give them one or more orders or bills of exchange on the tax receiver in Châlons, payable to their order. Let them endorse or pass their order to the Châlons wine merchants. These will obtain 50,000 livres from the receiver in Châlons. In this way the 50,000 livres in Paris will be paid to the tax farms' cashier in Paris, and the 50,000 livres in Châlons will be paid to the wine merchants [327] of this city. The trouble of transporting this silver from one city to another is avoided by this exchange or offset. Alternatively, the Châlons wine merchants who have 50,000 livres in Paris may go and offer their bills of exchange to the receiver, who will endorse them to the tax farms' cashier in Paris, who will cash them there, and let the receiver in Châlons pay them the 50,000 livres that he has there for their bills of exchange. Whichever way this offset is made, by either drawing the Parisian bills of exchange on Châlons, or drawing the Châlons bills on Paris, the exchange is said to be at par since, in this instance, ounce for ounce is paid, and 50,000 livres for 50,000 livres.

The same method may be applied between these wine merchants [328] in Châlons and the rent collectors for the nobility in Paris, who have lands or rents in the area of Châlons, and again between the wine merchants, or all other merchants in Châlons, who have sent commodities or merchandise to Paris and who have money there, and all the merchants who have purchased merchandise in Paris and sold it in Châlons. If there is a sizable trade between these two cities, bankers will emerge in Paris and in Châlons who will negotiate with the interested parties on both sides and will be the agents or the intermediaries for the payments that would have to be sent from one of these cities to the other. Now if all the wines and other commodities and merchandise that have been sent from Châlons to Paris and effectively sold there for cash exceed by 5,000 ounces of silver, or 25,000 livres, the [329] tax receipts in Châlons, the rents that the nobility in Paris receive from the district of Châlons, and even the value of all the commodities and merchandise that were sent from Paris to Châlons and sold there for cash, the Parisian banker will necessarily have to send that amount in money to Châlons. This amount will be the excess or the balance of trade between these two cities. It will, I contend, be necessarily sent in specie to Châlons, and this operation will be carried out in the following or related manner.

The agents or correspondents of the Châlons wine merchants and others who have sent commodities or merchandise from Châlons to Paris [330] have the money from these sales in cash at Paris. They have orders to remit it to Châlons. But as they normally do not risk sending it by carriage, they will apply to the tax farms' cashier, who will give them orders or bills of exchange on the tax farmer in Châlons, up to the limit of the funds that he has in Châlons, and this usually at par. But as they also need to remit other amounts to Châlons, they will apply for this to the banker, who will have at his disposal the rents of the nobles in Paris who have lands in the district of Châlons. This banker, in a similar way to that of cashier for the tax farms, will furnish them with bills of exchange, drawn on his correspondent in Châlons, up to the limit of the funds available to him in Châlons that he has been ordered to remit to Paris. This offset [331] will also be made at par, but for the fact that the banker attempts to make a small profit for his trouble, as much from the agents who ask him to send their money to Châlons as from the nobles who charged him to send their money from Châlons to Paris. If the banker also has at his disposal in Châlons money for the value of merchandise sent there from Paris, he will again provide bills of exchange for this amount.

But in our example the Parisian agents of the Châlons merchants are still holding 25,000 livres in Paris, over and above all the amounts mentioned previously, which they have been ordered to remit to Châlons. If they offer this money to the cashier for the tax farms, he will reply [332] that he has no further funds in Châlons and that he cannot furnish them with bills of exchange or orders on this city. If they offer the money to the banker he will tell them that he has no more funds in Châlons and that he has no opportunity to draw, but that he will be prepared to furnish bills if they are willing to pay him 3 percent. They will offer him 1 or 2 percent, and finally, not being able to do better, 2½ percent. At this price the banker will consent to give them bills; that is, by paying him 2 livres 10 sols in Paris, he will provide a bill of exchange for 100 livres, drawn on his correspondent in Châlons, payable in ten or fifteen days so as to enable his correspondent in Châlons to be in a position to pay the 25,000 livres that he draws on him. At this rate of exchange he will send this amount to him in gold specie [333] by the post messenger or stagecoach, or in default of gold, in silver. He will pay 10 livres for each bag of 1,000 livres, or, in bankers' language, 1 percent. He will pay a commission of 5 livres per bag of 1,000 livres to his correspondent in Châlons, or ½ percent, and he will keep for his own profit 1 percent. On this basis the exchange at Paris for Châlons is 2½ percent above par, because 2 livres 10 sols are paid for each 100 livres as the price on exchange.

In roughly this way, through the intermediation of bankers, and generally for large amounts, the balance of trade is transacted from one city to another. Not all of those who bear the title of banker carry out these transactions, and many of them are involved only in commissions and bank speculations. I will include as [334] bankers only those who remit money. It is up to them always to fix the exchanges, the prices of which are determined by the costs and risks of transporting specie in the different cases.

The rate of exchange between Paris and Châlons is rarely fixed at more than 2½ or 3 percent above or below par. But from Paris to Amsterdam, the rate of exchange will rise to 5 or 6 percent when it is necessary to transport specie. The distance is longer, the risk is greater, and more correspondents and agents are needed. The price of transport will be 10 to 12 percent from the Indies to England. In peacetime the rate of exchange seldom exceeds 2 percent between London and Amsterdam.

In our current example it will be said in Paris that the exchange for Châlons is at 2½ percent above par. [335] In Châlons it will be said that the exchange on Paris is at 2½ percent below the par because, in these circumstances, whoever pays cash in Châlons for a bill of exchange for Paris will give only 97 livres and 10 sols in order to receive 100 livres in Paris. It is evident that the city, or place, where the exchange is above the par is in debt to where it is below par, as long as the exchange rate remains on this basis. The exchange at Paris is at 2½ percent above par for Châlons only because Paris is in debt to Châlons, and the money corresponding to this debt needs to be transported from Paris to Châlons. For this reason it may be concluded that, when the exchange rate of a city is commonly above the par relative to another, the first city [336] owes a balance of trade to the second. When the exchange rates in Madrid or Lisbon are above par for all other countries, this shows that these two capitals must always send specie to these other countries.

In all the markets and cities that use the same money and the same gold and silver specie, such as Paris and Châlons sur Marne, and London and Bristol, the exchange rate is known and expressed as giving and taking so much percent above or below the par. When 98 livres are given in one place to receive 100 livres in another place, it is said that the exchange is about 2 percent below the par. When 102 livres are paid in a place to receive just 100 in another place, it is said that the exchange [337] is at exactly 2 percent above the par. When 100 livres are given in one place to receive 100 livres in another place, it is said that the exchange is at par. There is no difficulty or mystery in all of this.

But when the exchange is determined between two cities or markets where the money is altogether dissimilar, where the coins are of differing sizes, fineness, or make and even have different names, the nature of exchange initially appears to be more difficult to explain. But essentially this foreign exchange differs from that between Paris and Châlons only in terms of the jargon that the bankers use. The exchange between Paris and Holland is quoted by stipulating the écu of 3 livres against so many Dutch deniers de gros. But the parity of exchange between Paris and Amsterdam is always 100 ounces of [338] gold or silver against 100 ounces of gold or silver of the same weight and fineness. Thus, 102 ounces paid in Paris to receive only 100 ounces in Amsterdam still comes to 2 percent above the par. The banker who arranges the remittances of the balance of trade must always be able to calculate the par. But in the language of foreign exchange, the price of exchange in

London with Amsterdam will be quoted by giving 1 pound sterling in London to receive 35 Dutch escalins at the bank; with Paris by giving 30 deniers or pennies sterling in London to receive in Paris an écu or 3 livres tournois. Such descriptions do not indicate whether the exchange is above or below par. But the banker who remits the balance of trade knows exactly the account, and how much he will receive [339] in foreign specie in return for that of his own country that he transfers.

Whether the exchange in London is fixed for English money in Moscovite rubles, in mark lubs of Hamburg, in German rixdollars, in Flemish livres de gros, in Venetian ducats, in piastres of Genoa or Leghorn, in Portugese millreis or crusadoes, in Spanish pieces of eight, or pistoles, and so forth, the exchange parity for all countries will always be 100 ounces for 100 ounces of gold and silver. If in the language of exchange it is found that more or less than this par is given, it comes to the same thing as if it was said that the exchange is so much above or below par. It will always be known whether or not England owes the balance to the market in which the exchange rate is settled, just as it [340] was known in our example of Paris and Châlons.

3

*Further explanations toward
an understanding of the nature
of exchanges*

It has been shown that the exchanges are determined by the intrinsic value of specie, that is, at par, and that their difference comes from the costs and risks of transport from one place to another when the balance of trade has to be sent in specie. It is unnecessary to reason about something that may be seen plainly in fact and in practice. Bankers sometimes introduce refinements into this practice.

If England owes France 100,000 ounces of silver for [341] the balance of trade, if France owes 100,000 ounces to Holland, and Holland 100,000 ounces to England, all these three sums may be offset by bills of exchange between the respective bankers of these three states without the need to send silver on any side.

If in the month of January Holland sends merchandise worth 100,000 ounces of silver to England, and England, in this same month, sends merchandise worth only 50,000 ounces (I assume that in the same month of January the sale and payment are made by both sides), Holland will be due a balance of trade of 50,000 ounces in this month and the Amsterdam exchange will be at 2 or 3 percent [342] above the par in the month of January; that is to say in exchange language that the Dutch exchange, which was at par, or at 35 escalins in London, will rise to roughly 36 escalins in January. But when the bankers send this debt of 50,000 ounces to Holland, the Amsterdam exchange will naturally fall back to par, or 35 escalins, in London.

But if an English banker foresees in January, due to the export of an extraordinary quantity of merchandise to Holland, that Holland will owe a great deal to England during the payment and sales in March, he may from the month of January furnish bills of exchange [343] for the amount of value to be paid on maturity, drawn on his Amsterdam correspondent, payable at double usance or two months instead of sending the 50,000 écus or ounces that he owes that month to Holland. In this way he profits on the exchange that was at par in January and will be below par in March and gains doubly without sending a sol to Holland.

This is called speculation by the bankers, who often cause short-term changes in the exchange independently of the balance of trade. But in the long term it is necessary to return to this balance, which sets the constant and uniform rule of exchange. Although the bankers' speculations and credits may sometimes delay the transport of sums owing from one city or state to another, it is always ultimately necessary to pay the debt and to send the balance of trade in specie [344] to the place where it is due.

If England continually gains a balance of trade with Portugal and always loses a balance with Holland, the exchange rates with Holland and Portugal will make this clear. It will be seen that in London the exchange for Lisbon is always below par and that Portugal is indebted to England. It will also be seen that the exchange for Amsterdam is above par and that England is indebted to Holland. It is not possible, however, to determine the quantity of the debt by the exchanges. It cannot be seen whether the balance of money withdrawn from Portugal will be greater or smaller than that needed to be sent to Holland.

One thing, however, will always be known in London, whether England gains or loses the general balance of [345] its trade (by general balance is meant the net balance of trade with all the foreign states that trade with England), and that is the price of gold and silver bullion, but particularly that of gold (given that today the proportion of the price of gold and silver in coinage differs from the proportion of the market price, as will be explained in the next chapter). If the price of gold bullion in the London market, which is the center of English trade, is lower than the price at the Tower [of London], where guineas or gold coins are minted, or at the same price as these coins intrinsically, and if gold bullion is brought to the Tower in order to obtain its value in guineas or minted coins, this is a certain proof that England gains in its general balance of trade. [346] It is proof that gold drawn from Portugal not only suffices to pay England's balance with Holland, Sweden, Moscow, and the other creditor states, but that there is still gold to send for minting to the Tower, and the quantity or amount of this general balance is known from that of the coins minted at the Tower of London.

But if gold bullion sells in the London market at a higher price than that of the Tower, which is normally £3 18s per ounce, the bullion will not be brought to the Tower for minting. This is a definite sign that not as much gold is drawn from abroad, for example from Portugal, as is necessary to send to the other countries to which England is indebted. This is a proof that the general balance of trade [347] is against England. This would not be known but for the prohibition on sending gold specie out of the kingdom. But this prohibition explains why the timid London bankers prefer to buy bullion (which they are allowed to transport abroad) at £3 18s up to £4 sterling an ounce to send abroad rather than to export illegally guineas or gold coins at £3 18s and risk their confiscation. Yet there are some who will take this risk, while others melt the gold coins to export them as bullion; it is thus impossible to estimate the quantity of gold that England loses when it faces an adverse general balance of trade.

In France the cost of minting, [348] usually 1½ percent, is deducted, that is, the price for coins is always higher than that for bullion. To determine if France loses its general balance of trade, it suffices to know if the bankers send French specie abroad. If they do, it is indeed proof that they cannot find bullion to buy for export, given that bullion, although at a lower price than specie in France, is of a greater value abroad, by at least 1½ percent.

Exchange rates rarely vary except in relation to the balance of trade between the state and other countries, and this balance is naturally only the difference between the value of the commodities and merchandise [349] exported by the state and those imported into the state. Yet frequently, circumstances and accidental causes, unrelated to the merchandise and trade, result in the transportation of considerable sums from one state to another. These causes influence the exchanges in the same way that the balance and the trade surplus would.

Examples of this are the sums of money that a state sends to another for its secret services or any foreign policy purposes; for subsidies to allies; for the upkeep of troops, ambassadors, traveling nobility, and the like; the capital sent by the inhabitants of one state to another to place in public or private capital there; the interest that these inhabitants annually [350] derive from such funds; and so forth. The exchanges inevitably vary as a result of all these accidental causes and follow the rule for the transport of silver that is needed. These types of issues are not dealt with separately, and indeed that would be difficult when analyzing the balance of trade. They most certainly have an influence on the increase and decrease of money in a state, and on its comparative strength and power.

My subject does not allow me to expand on the effects of these accidental causes. I will always confine myself to the simple views of trade, lest I further complicate my subject, which is already complex due to the multiplicity of facts relating to it.

Exchange rates rise more or less above the par in proportion to the greater or lower costs and risk of transporting silver. [351] Given this, the exchanges rise much more naturally above par in the cities and states where there are prohibitions on the transport of silver outside the state than in those where there are none.

Assume that Portugal each year regularly consumes considerable quantities of woolen and other manufactures from England, as much for its own people as for those of Brazil; that it pays for part of them with wine, oils, and the like, but for the surplus payment a regular balance of trade is sent from Lisbon to London. If the king of Portugal not only introduces severe penalties threatening confiscation, but also introduces the death penalty for those exporting any gold or silver bullion out of his states, the fear of these penalties will first of all stop the bankers [352] from sending the balance. The money arising from English sales will be kept in Lisbon. The English merchants, unable to obtain their money from Lisbon, will no longer send cloth there. This will cause cloth to become extraordinarily expensive. The cloth has not increased in price in England, however; it is just not sent to Lisbon because it is not possible to remit its value when sold. The Portuguese nobility and others who cannot do without it will offer to double the normal price for it. But as it is possible to obtain enough of it only by sending money out of Portugal, the increase in the price of cloth will become the profit of whoever will illegally send gold or silver out of the kingdom. This will encourage various Jews and others to bring gold and silver [353] to English vessels in Lisbon's harbor even at the risk of their lives. They will initially earn 50 to 100 percent in carrying out this business, a profit that is paid by the Portuguese people through the high prices that they pay for the cloth. Having successfully practiced it frequently, they will, little by little, become more adroit at this operation, and at length silver will be brought aboard the English ships for the price of 1 or 2 percent.

The king of Portugal enacts the law or the prohibition. His subjects, even his courtiers, pay the costs of the risk involved in making the prohibition useless and inoperable. No benefit is derived from such a law. On the contrary, it is really disadvantageous to Portugal because it is responsible for more money leaving the state than would leave in the absence of such a law.

[354] For those who gain from such an operation, be they Jews or

others, they will send their profits to foreign countries, and when they have had enough of it or when they become fearful they often follow their money.

If some of these offenders were caught in the act, had their assets confiscated, and were executed, this circumstance and execution, instead of stopping the export of money, would only increase it, because those who were previously happy with 1 or 2 percent to export silver would now look for 20 or 50 percent. Thus it is necessary for something always to be exported to pay the balance.

I do not know if I have succeeded in explaining these reasons to those who have no idea of trade. I know that nothing is easier to explain for those who have some practical knowledge [355] and that they are understandably astonished that those who direct the states and administer the finances of great kingdoms know so little about the nature of exchanges as to prohibit the export of bullion and gold and silver specie at the same time.

The only way to keep them in a state is to manage foreign trade so successfully that there is no adverse balance to the state.

4
Of the changes in the proportion of values relative to metals that are used as money

If metals were as easy to find as water commonly is, everyone would use [356] them for their needs, and these metals would have hardly any value. The metals that are the most abundant and cost the least trouble to produce are also the cheapest. Iron appears to be the most necessary, but, as it is commonly found in Europe with less trouble and labor than copper, it is much cheaper.

Copper, silver, and gold are the three metals commonly used as money. Copper mines are the most abundant and cost the least amount of land and labor to mine. Today Sweden has the richest copper mines.

More than 80 ounces of copper are needed to pay for 1 ounce of silver in the market. It is also pertinent to note that the copper drawn from certain mines is more perfect and [357] brighter than that taken from other mines. That of Japan and Sweden is brighter than that of England. In Roman times that of Spain was brighter than that of the island of Cyprus. Contrastingly, gold and silver, drawn from whatever mine, are always of the same quality when refined.

The value of copper, like anything else, is proportional to the land and labor that enter into its production. Aside from the ordinary uses to which it is put, such as pots, vases, kitchen utensils, locks, and so forth, it is used as money for small transactions in nearly all countries. In Sweden it is often used even for large payments when money is scarce there. During the first five centuries of Rome [358] it was the only money used. It was only in 484 that silver started to be used in exchange. The ratio of copper to silver was then stipulated by the mints at 72 to 1; in the coinage of 512 at 80 to 1; in the rating of 537 at 64 to 1; in the coinage of 586 at 48 to 1; in that of Drusus of 663 and that of Sylla of 672 at 53.3 to 1; in that of Mark Antony of 712 and that of Augustus of 784 at 56 to 1; in that of Nero of A.D. 54 at 60 to 1; in that of Antoninus of A.D. 160 at 64 to 1; in the time of Constantine A.D. 330 [359] at 120 to 125 to 1; in the century of Justinian around A.D. 550 at 100 to 1; and it has always varied below the ratio of 100 to 1 in all the European mints.

Today, copper is rarely used as money except for small transactions, either as in England when alloyed with calamine to produce yellow brass, or as in France and Germany when alloyed with a small amount of silver. It is generally valued at the ratio of 40 to 1, even though the market price for copper in terms of silver is at 80 and 100 to 1. The reason is that the cost of minting is normally deducted from the weight of the copper. Where there is insufficient amount of this change for the circulation of small transactions [360] in the state, copper money alone, or alloyed copper, is used without difficulty despite the deficiency in its intrinsic value. But when used for exchange with foreign countries it will be accepted only in terms of its copper weight and the silver weight that is alloyed with the copper. Even in states where, through either the greed or the ignorance of the rulers, too much of this small change is circulated in small transactions, and where it is or-dered that a certain amount be accepted for large transactions, it is not willingly accepted, and the small change stands at a discount to silver money. This is what happened to the brass money and ardites in Spain for large transactions. Small change, however, always trades without difficulty for minor transactions, [361] and the payments are normally for small amounts, so the corresponding loss is even smaller. This is the reason for their acceptability without difficulty and for the exchange-ability of copper for small silver coins above the copper's weight and intrinsic value within the state, but not with other states; each state possesses its own minting facilities to accommodate the range of its small transactions.

Gold and silver, like copper, have a value proportional to the land and labor necessary for their production. If the public authority takes care of the minting costs of these metals, their value in bullion bars and in coin is the same, and their market value and mint value are identical; their value in the state and in foreign countries is continually the same, always [362] determined according to weight and fineness, that is, by weight alone if these metals are pure and unalloyed.

Silver mines have always been found to be more abundant than those of gold, but not equally so across countries or across time. Several ounces of silver have always been required to pay for one ounce of gold, sometimes more and sometimes less, according to the abundance of these metals and demand for them. In the year A.U.C.[5] 310, 13 ounces of silver were needed in Greece to pay for an ounce of gold; that is, gold was to silver as 1 to 13; about A.U.C. 400 it was 1 to 12; in A.U.C. 460 it was 1 to 10 in both Greece and Italy and all of Europe. This ratio of 1 to 10 appears to have remained constant for three centuries until the [363] death of Augustus, in A.U.C. 767 or A.D. 14. Under Tiberius

5. A.U.C. stands for *anno urbis conditae,* or *ab urbe condita,* meaning in the year from the building of Rome. Cantillon used the building of Rome as the basis for the dates quoted in this paragraph. The building of Rome was dated as 753 B.C. This means that A.U.C. 310 translates into the year 443 B.C. Later in the paragraph there is the date A.U.C. 767 or A.D. 14. This is produced by subtracting 753 from 767 to give A.D. 14. —AEM

gold became scarcer, or silver became more abundant, the ratio rising gradually to 1 to 12, 12½, and 13. Under Constantine, A.D. 330, and under Justinian, A.D. 550, it was 1 to 14⅖. Since then history has been less revealing. Some believe that they discovered this ratio to be 1 to 18 for certain French kings. During the reign of Charles the Bald, in A.D. 840, gold and silver coins were minted and the ratio was 1 to 12. Under the reign of Saint Louis, who died in 1270, the ratio was 1 to 10; in 1361, 1 to 12; in 1421, [364] over 1 to 11; in 1500, below 1 to 12; around 1600, 1 to 12; in 1641, 1 to 14; in 1700, 1 to 15; in 1730, 1 to 14½.

The quantity of gold and silver, brought from Mexico and Peru in the last century, not only made these metals more abundant, but even raised the value of gold against the more plentiful silver, so that the Spanish mints, following the market prices, fixed the ratio at 1 to 16. The other European countries at their mints followed closely the Spanish price, some fixing it at 1 to 15⅝, the others at 1 to 15¾, 1 to 15⅝, etc., according to the judgments and views of the mint directors. [365] But ever since Portugal has drawn considerable quantities of gold from Brazil, the ratio has started to fall again, if not at the mints then at least in the market prices that apportion a greater value to silver than in the past. Besides, a great deal of gold is often brought from the East Indies in exchange for European silver because the ratio is far lower in the Indies.

In Japan, where there are many rich mines, the ratio of gold to silver is 1 to 8 today; in China, 1 to 10; in the other countries of the Indies on this side, 1 to 11, 1 to 12, 1 to 13, and 1 to 14, as we move closer to the West and Europe. But if the Brazilian [366] mines continue to supply so much gold, the ratio will probably easily fall in the long run to 1 to 10 even in Europe, which appears to me to be the most natural if there is something other than chance that guides this ratio. It is clearly evident that at the time when the gold and silver mines in Europe, Asia, and Africa were the most developed for the Roman Republic's account, the 1 to 10 ratio was the most constant.

If all the gold mines continually yielded a tenth of that produced by the silver mines, this would not suffice to infer that the ratio between the two metals would be one-tenth. This ratio is always dependent on demand and the market price. It could happen that rich people [367] might prefer to have gold coins rather than silver in their pockets and might develop a taste for gildings and gold ornaments in preference to those of silver, thereby increasing the market price of gold.

Additionally, it is not possible to determine the ratio for these metals by considering the quantity of them that are found in a state. Let us assume that the ratio is 1 to 10 in England and that the quantity of gold and silver circulating there amounts to 20 million ounces of silver and 2 million ounces of gold, the equivalent of 40 million ounces of silver, and that 1 million of the 2 million ounces of gold are exported from England in return for 10 million ounces of silver that are imported. There would then be 30 million ounces of silver and only 1 million ounces of gold, which is always the equivalent of 40 million ounces of silver. Measuring in terms of the quantity of ounces, there are 30 million ounces of silver [368] and 1 million ounces of gold. Consequently, if the relative quantity of metal were the determining factor, the ratio of gold to silver would be 1 to 30, but that is impossible. As the neighboring countries' ratio is 1 to 10 it will then cost only 10 million ounces of silver, along with some minor transport costs, to bring 1 million ounces of gold back into the state in return for 10 million ounces of silver.

The market price is decisive in establishing the ratio of gold to silver: the price is determined by the number of those who need one metal [369] in exchange for the other, and those who wish to carry out this exchange. The ratio frequently depends on people's opinion: the bargaining is carried out roughly and not geometrically. I do not, however, believe that it is possible to imagine any rule other than this to arrive at the ratio. At least in practice we know that this is the determinant, as is the case for the price and value of everything else. Foreign markets influence the price of gold and silver more than the price of any other commodity or merchandise because they may be transported so easily and without damage. If there were a free and regular trade between England and Japan, if a number of ships were continually used for this trade and the balance of [370] trade were equal in all respects, that is, having regard to price and value a similar amount of merchandise was continually exported from England to Japan as was imported in merchandise from Japan, all the gold from Japan would be drawn in exchange for silver in the long run, and the ratio between gold and silver in Japan would be made equivalent to that in England, with the one difference being that of the shipping risk, because in our example the costs of transport would be borne by the trade in merchandise.

Allowing for the 1 to 15 ratio in England and that of 1 to 8 in Japan, there would be 87 percent to gain by sending English silver to Japan and by bringing back gold. But this does not usually suffice to pay [371] for the costs of such a long and difficult voyage. It is better to bring back Japanese merchandise paid in silver rather than returning with gold. In different states only the costs and risks of transporting gold and silver can produce a difference in the ratio of these metals. In the nearest state the ratio will differ very little; there will be a difference of 1, 2, or 3 percent between one state and another, and between England and Japan the sum of all these differences in the ratio will rise to above 87 percent.

It is the market price that determines the ratio of the value of gold to silver. The market price is the basis for this proportion in the value given to gold and silver coins. If the market price varies considerably, [372] the coinage will need to be reformed to follow the market rate. If this is not done, the circulation will be confused and disordered, and coins of one or the other metal will be sold at a higher price than that fixed by the mint. Antiquity provides an infinity of examples of this; recently there has been one in England due to the London mint's laws. The ounce of silver eleven-twelfths fine is worth 5s 2d there. Since the ratio of gold to silver (that had been fixed at 1 to 16 in imitation of Spain) had fallen to 1 to 15 and 1 to 14½, the ounce of silver sold at 5s 6d while the golden guinea's market price continued to be 21s 6d. [373] This caused all the unworn silver crowns, shillings, and sixpences to be exported from England. Silver became so scarce in 1728 (though only the most worn coins continued to be used) that it was necessary to change the guinea at a loss of almost 5 percent. The disorder and confusion produced by this in trade and circulation obliged the treasury to request the renowned Sir Isaac Newton, director of the Tower Mint, to report on the most suitable measures to address this disorder.

Nothing could have been easier. All that was needed was to follow the market price of silver for minting silver coins at the Tower. Instead of using the gold-to-silver ratio [374] of 1 to 15¾ that had long been stipulated by the Tower Mint's regulations and laws, all that was needed was to mint lighter silver coins at the market ratio that had fallen below that of 1 to 15, and, anticipating the change that Brazilian gold annually brings in the ratio of these two metals, it might even have been possible to establish it on the basis of 1 to 14½, as was done in France in 1725, and as they will be forced to follow later in England.

It is true that one can equally adjust the English coinage to the market price and ratio by reducing the nominal value of gold coins. This was the approach taken by Sir [Isaac] Newton [375] in his report, and by Parliament resulting from his report. But, as I hope to explain, this was the least natural and most disadvantageous approach. First, it was more natural to raise the price of silver coins because the public had already raised them in the market, since the ounce of silver, valued at only 62 pence sterling at the Tower's price, was worth over 65 in the market, and all the unworn silver coins had been exported out of England. On the other hand, it was less disadvantageous for the English nation to raise silver coins than to lower those of gold, given the sums that England owes abroad.

If it is assumed that England [376] owes the foreigner 5 million sterling of capital that is invested in public funds, it may equally be assumed that the foreigner paid in gold for this capital at the rate of 21s and 6d for a guinea, or alternatively in silver at 65d sterling the ounce, according to the market price.

At 21s 6d to the guinea, these 5 million sterling have consequently cost the foreigner 4,651,163 guineas, but now that the guinea has been reduced to 21s it will be necessary, in order to repay this capital, to pay 4,761,904 guineas. This will constitute a loss of 110,741 guineas to England without counting the losses arising from the annual interest that is paid.

[377] Mr. Newton, in replying to this objection, told me that, following the fundamental laws of the kingdom, silver was the unique and true money, and as such it could not be changed.*

It is easy to reply that the public having changed this law by practice,

---

* Here Mr. Newton sacrificed the substance to the form.

and by the market price, it had ceased to be a law. In these circumstances it would be disadvantageous for the nation to adhere scrupulously to it and to pay foreigners more than they were owed. If gold coins had not been considered a true money, it would have supported the change as happens in Holland and in China, where gold is perceived more as a commodity than as money. If silver coins had been raised to the [378] market price, without touching gold, there would have been no loss to the foreigner, and there would have been an abundance of silver coins in circulation. They would have been minted at the Tower, whereas now none will be minted until a new arrangement is put in place.

Through the reduction in the value of gold from 21s 6d to 21s produced by Mr. Newton's report, an ounce of silver that sold before in the London market at 65 and 65½ pennies sold in truth at only 64 pence. But given the way it was minted at the Tower, the ounce was worth 64 in the market, and if it was brought to the Tower to be minted it was worth no more than 62, so no more was brought to it. A couple of shillings, or fifths of crowns, have been minted, losing on them the difference with the market price, at the expense [379] of the South Sea Company. But these disappeared as quickly as they were circulated. No silver coins containing the legal mint weight can be seen in circulation today. Only used and underweight—relative to their market price—silver coins are seen in exchange.

The market price of silver, however, continues to rise imperceptibly. The ounce that was only worth 64 after the reduction we have discussed has now risen again in the market to 65½ and 66. To have silver coins in circulation and minted at the Tower it will be necessary to reduce once again the value of the golden guinea, [380] from 21 shillings to 20 shillings, and lose double of what has already been lost to the foreigner, unless there is a preference to follow the natural course and to adjust silver coins to the market price. Only the market price can find the ratio of the value of gold to silver, as is the case for all other value ratios. Mr. Newton's reduction of the guinea to 21 shillings was devised only to prevent the disappearance of the light and used silver coins that remained in circulation. It was not designed to fix the true price ratio for gold and silver money. By the true ratio I mean that fixed by market prices. This price is always the touchstone in these matters. Changes in it are sufficiently slow to give [381] time to regulate the mints and to prevent disorders in the circulation.

In some centuries the value of silver against gold rises slowly. In others the value of gold rises against silver. This was the case in the age of Constantine, who reduced all values to that of gold as the more permanent. But the value of silver is usually the more permanent, and gold is more subject to change.

5

Of the augmentation and diminution of the denominational value of coin

According to the principles that have been established, the quantities of silver circulating [382] in exchange fix and determine all prices in a state, taking into account the rapidity or slowness of circulation.

During the augmentations and diminutions practiced in France, however, such strange changes are so frequently witnessed that it is possible to conceive that the market prices correspond more to the nominal value of coins than to their quantity in exchange: to the quantity of livres tournois in money of account rather than to the quantity of marks and ounces. This appears to be directly opposed to our principles.

Let us assume, as was the case in 1714, that the ounce of silver or écu legally exchanges for 5 livres and that the king publishes an *arrêt,* which orders the reduction of écus by 1 percent per month, [383] for a period of twenty months, to 4 livres instead of 5 livres. Taking into account the spirit of the nation, let us see the consequences that will naturally arise from this.

During the diminutions, all those who owe silver will hasten to pay it so as not to lose by them. The entrepreneurs and merchants find it easy to borrow money, allowing the least able and the least reputable to expand their businesses. They borrow money, as they believe, without interest and load themselves with merchandise at current prices. They even push up prices by the eagerness of their demands. Vendors have difficulty in getting rid of their merchandise for a money whose nominal value has to fall while they hold it. People turn toward foreign merchandise, [384] and considerable quantities amounting to the consumption of several years are imported. All of this increases the rapidity of the circulation of money and raises the prices of everything. These high prices prevent foreigners from importing their usual merchandise from France. France retains its own merchandise and at the same time imports sizable quantities of merchandise from abroad. This double operation results in the export of considerable quantities of specie to pay the balance.

The exchange rates will always show this disadvantage. The exchanges are commonly seen at 6 to 10 percent against France during the period of these diminutions. Enlightened people in France hoard their money during these same [385] times. The king finds the means of borrowing a great deal of money on which he willingly loses during the diminutions, proposing to compensate himself by an augmentation at the end of the diminutions.

With this end in view, after several diminutions, they start to hoard money in the king's coffers, delaying payments, pensions, and army pay. In these circumstances money becomes extremely scarce at the end of the diminutions, both because of the sums hoarded by the king and by various individuals, and because the nominal value of coins has been reduced. The sums sent abroad also contribute to the scarcity of money, and gradually this scarcity is the reason that the merchandise stocked by all the entrepreneurs is offered at 50 and 60 percent [386] discounts relative to those that were in place at the time of the first diminutions. Circulation is convulsed. Hardly enough money can be found to send to the market. Many entrepreneurs and merchants become bankrupt, and their merchandise is sold very cheaply.

Then the king once more augments the coinage, fixes the new écu, or the ounce of silver of the newly issued coins, at 5 livres. He starts to pay the troops and the pensions with these new coins. The older coins are demonetized and taken in only at the mint, at a lower nominal price, with the king profiting from the difference.

But all the sums of the new coinage created by the mint do not restore the abundance of money in circulation. The amounts hoarded by individuals and [387] those sent abroad greatly exceed the nominal increase of the coinage issued by the mint.

The cheapness of French merchandise starts to attract money from the foreigner, who, finding discounts of 50 and 60 percent and lower, sends gold and silver bullion to France to buy it. In this way the foreigner who sends his bullion to the mint is easily indemnified of the tax that he pays there on it. He has the double advantage of the cheap price of the merchandise that he purchases, and the loss of the mint tax really falls on the French in their sale of merchandise made abroad. They have enough merchandise for several years of consumption. For example, they resell to the Dutch [388] the spices that they themselves had imported from them at two-thirds of the original price that they paid. All of this happens slowly. Foreigners decide to buy this French merchandise only because of its cheapness. The balance of trade, which was against France at the time of the diminutions, turns in its favor at the time of the augmentation, and the king may profit by 20 percent or more on all the bullion brought into France and taken to the mint. As foreigners currently owe the balance of trade to France and as they have an insufficient amount of the newly issued coins, they need to bring their bullion and old coins to the mint to acquire new coins for payments. But this balance of trade, owed by foreigners to France, arises only [389] from the merchandise that they import cheaply.

France is all around the dupe in these operations. She pays very high prices for foreign merchandise during the diminutions. She resells it cheaply to these same foreigners during the augmentations. She sells cheaply her own merchandise, which she had kept so expensive during the diminutions. Thus it would be difficult for all the coins that left France during the diminutions to return there during the augmentation.

If, as nearly always happens, the coins of the new issue are counterfeited abroad, France loses the 20 percent mint tax established by the king. This is so much gained by the foreigner, who also profits from the cheap prices for merchandise in France.

[390] The king makes a considerable profit through the mint tax, but it costs France three times more for him to make this profit.

It is well understood that during the period when there is a current balance of trade in favor of France against foreigners, the king is in a position to raise a tax of 20 percent or more through a new issue of coins and by an increase in their nominal value. But if, during this new coinage and augmentation, the balance of trade is against France, this operation will not succeed, and the king will not derive a great profit from it. The reason is that in these circumstances it is continually necessary to send money abroad. But in foreign countries the old écu is as good as the newly minted écu. This being the case, the [391] Jews and bankers will give a premium or a secret bonus for the old coins, and the individual who can sell them above the mint price will not bring them there. He will only be given about 4 livres for his écu at the mint, but the banker will initially give him 4 livres 5 sols, then 4 livres 10, and finally 4 livres 15. This is the way in which a specie augmentation may fail. This can hardly happen when an augmentation is introduced after the indicated diminutions, because then the balance naturally turns in favor of France in the way that has been explained.

The experience of the 1726 augmentation may serve to confirm all of this. The diminutions preceding this augmentation were made [392] suddenly and without warning. This prevented the balance of trade from turning strongly in France's favor during the augmentation of 1726. Additionally, few people brought their old coins to the mint, and it was necessary to forget about the anticipated profit from the mint tax.

It is not within my subject to explain the ministers' reasons for the sudden diminution of the coinage, or those that misled them in their project for the augmentation of 1726. I wish only to discuss the French augmentations and diminutions because the effects that flow from them appear sometimes to run counter to the principles that I have established, namely that the abundance or scarcity of money in a state raises or lowers all prices proportionally.

[393] Having explained the effects of the diminutions and augmentations of the coinage as practiced in France, I maintain that they neither destroy nor weaken my principles. If I am told that what cost 20 livres or 5 ounces of silver before the specified diminutions does not even cost 4 ounces or 20 livres of newly issued money after the aug-

mentation, I will agree with this without straying from my principles, because, as I have explained, there will be less money in circulation than there was before the diminutions. The difficulties in exchange during the period and the operations under discussion cause changes in the prices of things and in the rate of interest, which cannot be taken as the rule in the ordinary principles of circulation and exchange.

The change in the nominal value [394] of specie has always been the effect of some misfortune or scarcity in the state, or of the ambition of some prince or individual. In the Roman year of 157, after an insurrection and the abolition of debts, Solon augmented the nominal value of the Athenian drachma. Between the Roman years of 490 and 512 the Roman republic augmented, a number of times, the nominal value of its copper money so that their *as* came to be worth 6. The pretext was to provide for the state's needs and to pay the debts that it had accrued from the time of the first Punic War. This caused a considerable amount of confusion. In 663 the People's Tribune, Livius Drusus, augmented the nominal value of silver coins by an eighth while reducing their fineness by as much. This resulted in the counterfeiters causing confusion [395] in exchange. In 712 Mark Antony, during his triumvirate, augmented, by mixing iron with silver, the nominal value of silver by 5 percent so as to meet the needs of the triumvirate. Since then many emperors have weakened or augmented the nominal value of the coinage. At different times the kings of France did likewise. This is why the livre tournois, which was usually worth 1 pound weight of silver, has fallen in value so little. This always caused disorder in states. The nominal value of the coinage is a matter of indifference, providing that it be permanent. The Spanish pistole is worth 9 livres or florins in Holland, about 18 livres in France, 37 livres 10 sols in Venice, and 50 livres in Parma. [396] Values between these different countries are exchanged in the same proportion. All prices increase gradually when the nominal value of coins increases. The actual quantity in terms of the weight and fineness of the coins, allowing for the rapidity of circulation, is the base and the determinant of values. A state neither gains nor loses from the raising or lowering of its coins as long as it maintains the same quantity of them, even though individuals may gain or lose from the change according to their obligations. People are full of false opinions and ideas as to the nominal value of their coins. We showed in the chapter dealing with exchanges that the certain rule for them is the price and fineness of the current coins of different countries, mark for mark, ounce for ounce. If an increase [397] or decrease of the nominal value changes this rule for some time in France, it is only during a crisis or a difficulty in trade. There is always a gradual return to the intrinsic value to which prices are necessarily brought both in the market and in the foreign exchanges.

6

Of banks and their credit

If 100 thrifty nobles or landlords, who annually save money for occasional land purchases, each lodge 10,000 ounces of silver with a London goldsmith or banker, so as to avoid the trouble of minding this money [398] at home and to prevent it from being stolen, they will receive in return from them notes payable on demand. They will often leave it there for a long time and, even when they have made a purchase, they will give notice to the banker a long time in advance to have their money ready when the delays involving deliberations and legal documents have been settled.

In these circumstances the banker will often be in a position to lend 90,000 ounces (of the 100,000 that he owes) throughout the year and will need to keep only 10,000 ounces in cash to meet any withdrawals. He does business with rich and thrifty clients so that as quickly as he is asked for 1,000 ounces from one side, 1,000 is brought from another side. Normally it suffices for him [399] to keep in cash one-tenth of what is deposited with him. There have been some examples and confirmations of this in London. Instead of the individuals in question keeping the greatest part of the 100,000 ounces in cash during the year, the practice of depositing it with a banker enables 90,000 of the 100,000 ounces to be put into circulation. This, first and foremost, encapsulates the idea that may be formed of the utility of these types of banks. The bankers or goldsmiths contribute to an acceleration in the circulation of money. They lend it out at interest at their own risk and peril, and yet they are, or have to be, always ready to pay their notes when presented on demand.

If an individual has 1,000 ounces to pay to another, he will give him the banker's [400] note in payment for this sum. Perhaps this other person will not ask for money from the banker. He will keep the note and will give it on occasion to a third person in payment. This note may pass through several hands for large payments without anyone requesting money from the banker for a long time. Only some, who are not perfectly confident or have several small sums to pay, will demand the whole sum. In this first example the banker's cash constitutes only a tenth part of his trade.

If 100 individuals, or landlords, deposit their income as it is paid with a banker every six months, and then require their money according to their need to spend it, the banker will, at the start of the half years, be in a position to lend for a short term of some months a great deal [401] more of the money that he owes and receives than he will be at the end of these periods. His experience of the behavior of his clients will teach him that he can hardly lend during the year more than a half of the sums that he owes. These types of bankers will find their credit ruined if they fail for an instant to pay their notes on their first presentation. When they are short of cash they will give anything to have money quickly; that is, they will pay a higher rate of interest than they receive for the sums that they have lent. Given this, their experience teaches them to keep sufficient in cash—more rather than less—so as to be always able to meet their commitments. Hence bankers of this type (and [402] they are the most numerous) always keep in cash half of the sums deposited with them and lend the other half at interest and put it into circulation. In this second example the banker circulates his notes of 100,000 ounces or écus with 50,000 écus.

If the banker has a sizable flow of deposits and great credit, this increases confidence in his notes and reduces the demand for payment on them. But this delays his payments by only a few days or weeks when they fall into the hands of people not used to dealing with him. He must always guide himself by those who regularly entrust him with their money. If his notes fall into the hands of those in his own business, they will hastily withdraw the money from him.

[403] If the banker's depositors are entrepreneurs and merchants who lodge large sums daily and soon afterward withdraw them, it will often happen that if the banker converts to his own use more than a third of his cash, he will find it difficult to meet their demands.

These illustrations make it easy to understand that the sums of money that a goldsmith or a banker may lend at interest or divert from his cash are naturally proportioned to the practice and conduct of his clients, and that while it has been seen that there are bankers who can manage with a cash reserve of one-tenth, others can scarcely operate with less than a half or two-thirds, even though their credit may be as well regarded as that of the first.

Some trust one banker, others another. The happiest [404] is the banker whose clients are rich nobles always seeking sound investments for their money without wishing, while waiting, to lodge it at interest.

A general and national bank has this advantage over an individual goldsmith's bank in that there is always greater confidence in it, the biggest deposits are always willingly brought to it even from the most distant quarters of the city, and it usually leaves to the smaller bankers only the deposits of minor sums from their neighborhoods. In countries where the prince does not have absolute authority, even the state's revenues are brought to it. This serves only to increase credit and confidence rather than injure them.

If the payments of a national bank are made by book credits or transfers, the advantage is that they will not be [405] subject to forgeries, whereas if the bank issues notes they may be counterfeited and cause trouble. There will also be the disadvantage that those who live in areas of the city distant from the bank, particularly those living in the countryside, will prefer to transact in silver rather than go there. On the other hand, if the notes of the bank circulate widely, they may be used far and near. The national banks of Venice and Amsterdam pay only through book credits, but that of London pays, according to the individuals' preference, by book credits, in banknotes, and in silver. At the moment it is also the strongest bank.

It will be understood, then, that the main advantage of banks in a city, both public and private, is to accelerate the circulation of money and to prevent too much of it from [406] being hoarded, as would naturally be the case for several time intervals.

7 *Other insights and inquiries concerning the utility of a National Bank*

It is of little importance to examine why the Bank of Venice, or that of Amsterdam, keeps its books in monies of account different from current money, and that there is always a transaction charge to convert these book credits into current money. This is not a point that has any consequence for circulation. The London Bank [Bank of England] has not followed its example. Its book accounts, notes, and payments are made and kept in current coin. This appears to me to be more [407] uniform, more natural, and no less useful.

I have been unable to obtain exact information on the quantity of sums normally brought to these banks, the total amount of their notes and accounts, the loans that they make, or the amounts that they usually hold as cash to meet demands. Someone more knowledgeable about these will be better able to discuss them. However, since I know fairly well that these sums are not as great as is commonly believed, I will not go to the trouble of further discussing them.

If the notes and accounts of the London Bank [Bank of England], which appear to me to be greater, rise from week to week to 4 million ounces of silver or about 1 million sterling, and if they are happy [408] to keep continually cash reserves of one-quarter, or £250,000 sterling, or 1 million ounces of silver in coin, the utility of this bank for circulation corresponds to an increase in the state's money of 3 million ounces, or £750,000 sterling, which is undoubtedly a considerable sum and of great utility for circulation in circumstances where this circulation needs to be accelerated; I have remarked elsewhere that there are cases where it is better for the state to slow rather than to accelerate circulation. I have heard it said that the notes and accounts of the London Bank [Bank of England] have risen in certain cases to 2 million sterling, but this appears to me to have been due only to an extraordinary accident. I think that this bank's [409] utility solely corresponds in general to about a tenth part of all the circulating money in England.

If the explanations that I was given in round figures on the Bank of Venice's income in 1719 are correct, it may be said that in general the utility of national banks never corresponds to the tenth part of the current money that circulates in a state. This is approximately what I learned there.

The state of Venice's revenues may annually amount to 4 million ounces of silver that need to be paid into accounts at the Bank. The collectors established for this purpose, who collect the taxes in money in Bergamo and in the most distant areas, are obliged to convert them into bank accounts when they make payments of them to the republic.

[410] In Venice it is a legal requirement that all payments above a certain small sum for negotiations, purchases, and sales must be made through the accounts of the bank. All the retailers who have collected current money in exchange find themselves obliged to acquire bank accounts so as to make large payments. Those who need to take back money for their own expenditure, or for small retail transactions, need to convert their bank accounts into current money.

It has been found that the buyers and sellers of bank accounts regularly balance when the books of the Bank do not exceed the value of 800,000 ounces of silver or thereabouts.

According to my informant, [411] the Venetians gained this knowledge through time and experience. When the Bank was first established, individuals brought their money to the Bank so as to have bank credits for the same value. This money deposited at the Bank was later spent for the needs of the republic. However, the bank accounts maintained their original value because there were as many people who needed to deposit as to withdraw. Then the state, in need of funds, gave bank credits to the war contractors instead of silver and doubled the amount of these credits.

Then, the number of sellers of bank money exceeding the number of buyers, these bank accounts [412] sold at a discount to silver and lost

20 percent. Due to this discredit, the republic's revenue fell by a fifth, and the only remedy found for this disorder was to pledge part of the state's assets so as to borrow through bank accounts bearing interest. Through the borrowing of these bank accounts half of them were canceled, and then, with the buyers and sellers of bank accounts almost balancing, the Bank regained its original credit, and the amount of bank accounts was found to have been reduced to 800,000 ounces of silver.

In this way the utility of the Bank of Venice relative to circulation corresponded to about 800,000 ounces of silver. If it is supposed that all the current money that circulates in the states of this republic [413] amounts to 8 million ounces of silver, the utility of the Bank corresponds to one-tenth of this silver.

A national bank in the capital of a great kingdom or state must appear to contribute less in assisting circulation, because of the distance of its provinces, than that of one in a small state. When money circulates in greater abundance there than in neighboring countries, a national bank causes more harm than good. An abundance of fictive and imaginary money causes disadvantages similar to those of an increase of real money in circulation, by raising the price of land and labor there, or by making works and manufactures more expensive at the risk of losing them later. But this furtive abundance disappears at the first whiff of discredit and precipitates disorder.

[414] In France, during the middle of Louis XIV's reign, more money was seen in circulation than in neighboring countries, and the prince's revenues were raised, without the assistance of a bank, as easily and expeditiously as those raised today in England with the assistance of the London Bank [Bank of England].

If, during one of its four fairs, the Lyons clearings amount to 80 million livres, and if they are initiated and ended with just 1 million of ready money, they are undoubtedly very convenient in economizing on a vast number of silver deliveries from one house to another. But with that proviso, it certainly appears feasible to carry out all [415] the payments of 80 million in three months with this same million of cash that had started and finished these clearings.

Parisian bankers have often remarked that the same sack of silver was returned to them four to five times in the same day when they had a great deal of payments to make and receive.

I believe the public banks to be of great utility in small states and in those where silver is somewhat scarce. But I believe them to be less useful for the solid advantage of a great kingdom.

The Emperor Tiberius, a strict and thrifty prince, amassed in the imperial treasury 2,700 million sesterces, corresponding to 25 million sterling or 100 million ounces of silver, a huge sum in coin for those times and even today. It is true that in hoarding so much silver [416] he interfered with the circulation, and silver became even scarcer in Rome than it had been.

Tiberius, attributing this scarcity to the monopolies of the business-people and financiers who farmed the empire's tax revenues, ordered by an edict that they should spend at least two-thirds of their funds in purchasing land. Instead of reviving circulation this edict created chaos. All the financiers hoarded and recalled their funds under the pretext of preparing to obey the edict by buying land, which instead of rising in price became much cheaper due to the scarcity of silver in circulation. Tiberius remedied this silver shortage by lending just 300 million sesterces to individuals on good security, that is, the ninth part of the coin in his treasury.

[417] If the ninth part of the treasury sufficed in Rome to reestablish circulation, it would appear that the establishment of a general bank in a great kingdom, where its utility would never correspond to the tenth part of the money in circulation when it is not hoarded, would be of no real or permanent benefit, and that considering it from the perspective of its intrinsic value, it may be regarded only as an expedient for gaining time.

But a real increase in the quantity of circulating silver is of a different nature. We have already discussed this and Tiberius's treasury presents another opportunity to talk about it. Left at the death of Tiberius, this treasury of 2,700 million sesterces was dissipated in less than a year by his successor, the emperor Caligula. [418] Money had never been so abundant in Rome. What was its effect? This amount of money plunged the Romans into luxury and into all sorts of crimes to obtain it. Every year more than 600,000 pounds sterling left the empire for the merchandise of the Indies. In less than thirty years the empire was impoverished, and without any dismemberment or loss of a province, money became very scarce in it.

Although I reckon that a general bank is fundamentally of very little permanent utility in a great state, I am prepared to allow that there are circumstances in which a bank may produce effects that appear astonishing.

In a city with considerable public indebtedness, the facility of a bank enables the instantaneous purchase and sale of capital [419] funds for sizable amounts without causing any disturbance to the circulation. If in London an individual sells his South Sea capital stock to buy other stock in the Bank or the Indies Company, or in the hope that in a short time he will be able to buy capital stock in the same South Sea Company at a lower price, he always uses banknotes. Normally silver is not demanded for these notes, except for the value of interest on them. As one seldom spends one's capital, there is no need to convert it into coin, but one is always obliged to ask the Bank for the money necessary for subsistence, because coins are needed for small transactions.

If a landlord [420] with 1,000 ounces of silver pays 200 of them for the interest on public funds and spends 800 ounces himself, the 1,000 ounces will always need to be in coin. This landlord will spend 800 of them and the owners of the funds will spend 200. But when these owners are used to stock jobbing, buying and selling public stocks, no ready money is needed for these operations. It suffices to have banknotes. If it were necessary to withdraw coins from circulation to use for these purchases and sales, it would amount to a considerable sum and would often interfere with the circulation, or rather, in this case, it would happen that it would not be possible to buy and sell these stocks so frequently.

Undoubtedly the origin of these capitals, or of the money [421] deposited at the Bank, is only rarely withdrawn, such as when the owner of stocks becomes involved in some small transaction that requires coin; that is the reason for the Bank holding cash of only one-quarter or one-sixth of the silver against which it issues notes. If the Bank had not the funds of many of these capitals, it would find itself during the normal course of circulation reduced like individual bankers to keeping half of the funds entrusted to it to meet demands on it. It is true that it is not possible, using the Banks' books and its transactions, to distinguish the quantity of these types of capital that pass through several hands in the sales and purchases that are made in Change Alley. These notes are often renewed at the Bank and exchanged against others in trade. But [422] experience of the purchases and sales of capital stocks clearly shows that the sum of them is considerable, and that without these purchases and sales the amounts on deposit at the Bank would easily be a great deal smaller.

In 1720 the capital of the public stocks and the bubbles that were snares and the businesses of individual companies in London rose to a value of 800 million sterling. The purchases and sales of such poisonous stocks, however, were easily transacted through the amount of notes of all kinds that were created, while the same paper money [423] was accepted in payment of interest. But as soon as the idea of immense fortunes encouraged many individuals to increase their expenditure, to buy carriages, foreign linen, and silks, coin was necessary for all of this—I mean for the expenditure of the interest—and this destroyed all the systems.

This example clearly shows that the paper and credit of public and private banks may produce surprising results in everything unconnected with the ordinary expenditure involved in drinking, eating, clothing, and other family necessities. But in the usual course of circulation, the assistance of banks and of credit of this type is a great deal smaller and less solid than is generally thought. Silver alone is the true sinew of circulation. [424]

8 *Of the refinements of credit of general banks*

The national Bank of London [Bank of England] is composed of a great number of shareholders who select directors to manage its operations. Their chief advantage consisted in making an annual distribution of the profits generated through the lending at interest of the funds deposited at the Bank. The public funds, on which the state pays an annual interest, were later incorporated with it.

Despite such a strong foundation, a run on the Bank was witnessed (when the Bank lent heavily to the state and the holders of banknotes feared that the Bank was in difficulties), [425] with those holding banknotes rushing in a crowd to the Bank to withdraw their silver. The same thing happened during the collapse of the South Sea in 1720.

The refinements introduced to support the Bank and alleviate its discredit involved at first the designation of a number of clerks to count silver to give to those presenting banknotes, to pay out sizable amounts in sixpences and shillings so as to gain time, and to pay some parts to individual holders who had been waiting in turn all day to be paid. But the biggest amounts were paid to friends who took them and then secretly returned them to the Bank, only to use the same ploy the next day. In this way the Bank presented a solid image and gained time while [426] waiting for the discredit to slow down. But when this did not suffice, the Bank opened up for subscriptions so as to bring reputable and solvent people together to act as guarantors for large amounts and to support the credit and circulation of the banknotes.

Through this last refinement the Bank's credit was maintained in 1720 during the collapse of the South Sea. The run on the Bank stopped and deposits were brought to it as usual, once the public learned that the subscription had been filled by rich and powerful men.

If a minister of state in England, seeking to lower the rate of interest on money, or for other reasons, forces up the prices of public stock in London, and if he has sufficient authority [427] over the directors of the Bank to encourage them (under the obligation of compensating them in case of loss) to issue further banknotes, for which there is no backing, begging them to use the notes themselves to purchase more blocks and capital of the public stock, the price of this stock will not fail to rise due to these operations. Those who sold them, seeing the continuation of this high price, will perhaps decide—so as not to leave their banknotes idle and believing the rumors that have been spread that the interest rate will fall and that these stocks will rise again—to buy them at a higher price than that at which they sold them. If several

people, seeing the Bank's agents purchasing these funds, become involved in doing likewise, believing that they can profit as they do, the
public [428] stock will increase in price to the point that the minister
wishes. It may happen that the Bank will adroitly resell at the higher
price all the stocks that it bought at the minister's request and will not
only make a sizable profit, but will also retire and destroy all the excessive notes that it issued.

If, through its purchases, the Bank alone raises the price of public
stock, it will cause that price to fall by as much when it wishes to resell
it to cancel its excess note issue. But it always happens that many people, wishing to imitate the operations of the Bank's agents, help to sustain the price. Some even become entrapped because they do not understand these operations, where there is an infinity of refinements, or
rather chicanery, which are not part of my subject.

[429] It is then certain that a bank, in concert with a minister, is able
to increase and support the price of public stock and to lower the
state's rate of interest with the consent of this minister, when these
operations are discreetly managed and in this way free the state of its
debts. But these refinements, which open the door to making great fortunes, are rarely managed for the sole benefit of the state, and those
who operate them are often corrupted. The excessive banknotes that
are created and issued on these occasions do not disturb the circulation
because, as they are employed for the purchase and sale of capital stock,
they are not used for household expenditure and they are not converted
into silver. But if some fear or unforeseen accident drove the holders
[430] to demand silver at the bank, the bomb would explode, and it
would be seen that these are dangerous operations.

INDEX

This book is set in Garamond Premier Pro, a 1988 adaptation by Robert Slimbach of the typeface cut around 1540 by the French punchcutter, typographer, and printer Claude Garamond. The original Garamond face, with its small lowercase height and restrained contrast between thick and thin strokes, is a classic old-style face and has long been one of the most influential and widely used typefaces. Slimbach based the italic on type designed by Robert Granjon.

Printed on paper that is acid-free and meets the requirements of the American National Standard for Permanence of Paper for Printed Library Materials, z39.48-1992. ∞

Book design by Richard Hendel, Chapel Hill, North Carolina
Typography by Grapevine Publishing Services, Madison, Wisconsin
Printed and bound by Worzalla Publishing Company, Stevens Point, Wisconsin